Francis Frith's

Around

Peterborough

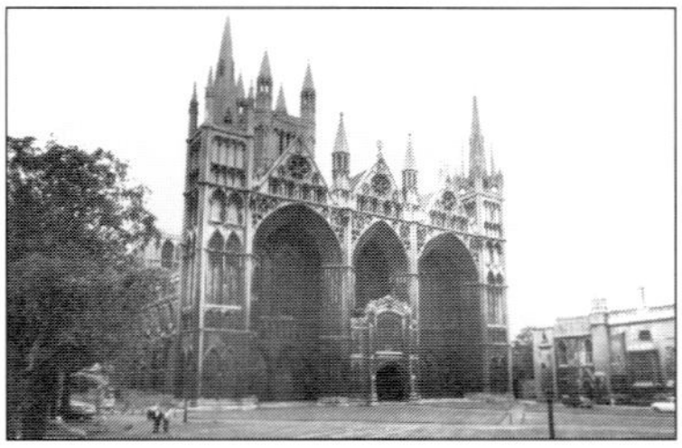

Photographic Memories

Francis Frith's Around Peterborough

Robert Cook

FRITH BOOK Co

Paperback edition first published in the United Kingdom in 2000 by
Frith Book Company Ltd

British Library Cataloguing in Publication Data

Francis Frith's Around Peterborough
Robert Cook
ISBN 1-85937-219-8

Frith Book Company Ltd
Frith's Barn, Teffont,
Salisbury, Wiltshire SP3 5QP
Tel: +44 (0) 1722 716 376
Email: info@frithbook.co.uk
www.frithbook.co.uk

Printed and bound in Great Britain

Front Cover: Long Causeway, 1904 51548

Dedicated to the late R G T Akins, true Fenlander and an inspiration.

AS WITH ANY HISTORICAL DATABASE THE FRITH ARCHIVE IS CONSTANTLY BEING CORRECTED AND IMPROVED AND THE PUBLISHERS WOULD WELCOME INFORMATION ON OMISSIONS OR INACCURACIES

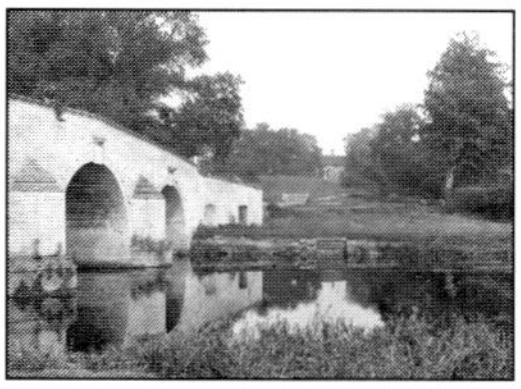

Contents

Francis Frith: *Victorian Pioneer*

Francis Frith, Victorian founder of the world-famous photographic archive, was a complex and multi-talented man. A devout Quaker and a highly successful Victorian businessman, he was both philosophic by nature and pioneering in outlook.

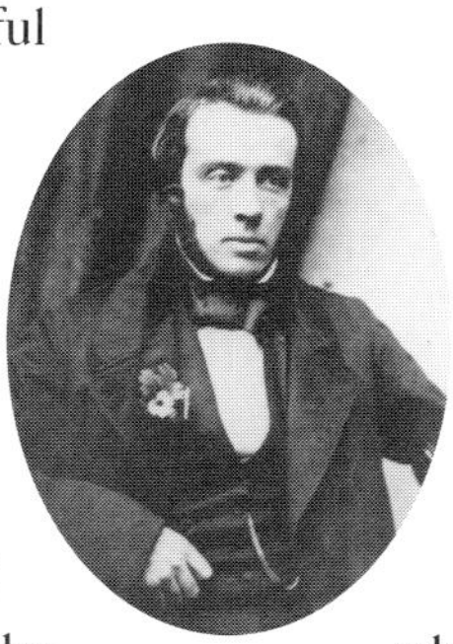

By 1855 Francis Frith had already established a wholesale grocery business in Liverpool, and sold it for the astonishing sum of £200,000, which is the equivalent today of over £15,000,000. Now a multi-millionaire, he was able to indulge his passion for travel. As a child he had pored over travel books written by early explorers, and his fancy and imagination had been stirred by family holidays to the sublime mountain regions of Wales and Scotland. 'What a land of spirit-stirring and enriching scenes and places!' he had written. He was to return to these scenes of grandeur in later years to 'recapture the thousands of vivid and tender memories', but with a different purpose. Now in his thirties, and captivated by the new science of photography, Frith set out on a series of pioneering journeys to the Nile regions that occupied him from 1856 until 1860.

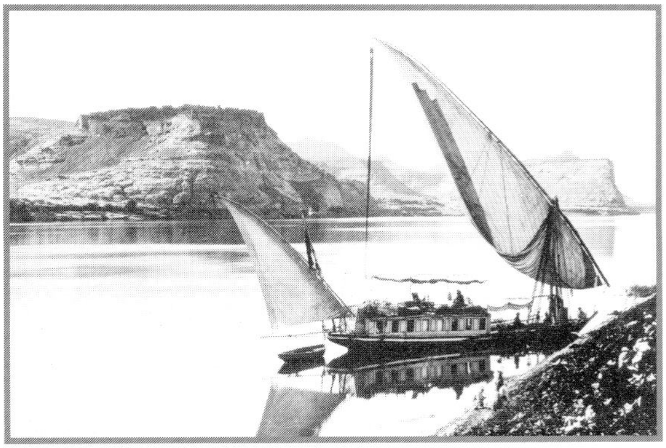

Intrigue and Adventure

He took with him on his travels a specially-designed wicker carriage that acted as both dark-room and sleeping chamber. These far-flung journeys were packed with intrigue and adventure. In his life story, written when he was sixty-three, Frith tells of being held captive by bandits, and of fighting 'an awful midnight battle to the very point of surrender with a deadly pack of hungry, wild dogs'. Sporting flowing Arab costume, Frith arrived at Akaba by camel seventy years before Lawrence, where he encountered 'desert princes and rival sheikhs, blazing with jewel-hilted swords'.

During these extraordinary adventures he was assiduously exploring the desert regions bordering the Nile and patiently recording the antiquities and peoples with his camera. He was the first photographer to venture beyond the sixth cataract. Africa was still the mysterious 'Dark Continent', and Stanley and Livingstone's historic meeting was a decade into the future. The conditions for picture taking confound belief. He laboured for hours in his wicker dark-room in the sweltering heat of the desert, while the volatile chemicals fizzed dangerously in their trays. Often he was forced to work in remote tombs and caves where conditions were cooler. Back in London he exhibited his photographs and was 'rapturously cheered' by members of the Royal Society. His reputation as a photographer was made overnight. An eminent modern historian has likened their impact on the population of the time to that on our own generation of the first photographs taken on the surface of the moon.

Venture of a Life-Time

Characteristically, Frith quickly spotted the opportunity to create a new business as a specialist publisher of photographs. He lived in an era of immense and sometimes violent change. For the poor in the early part of Victoria's reign work was a drudge and the hours long, and people had precious little free time to enjoy themselves. Most had no transport other than a cart or gig at their disposal, and had not travelled far beyond the boundaries of their own town or village. However, by the 1870s, the railways had threaded their way across the country, and Bank Holidays and half-day Saturdays had been made obligatory by Act of Parliament. All of a sudden the ordinary working man and his family were able to enjoy days out and see a little more of the world.

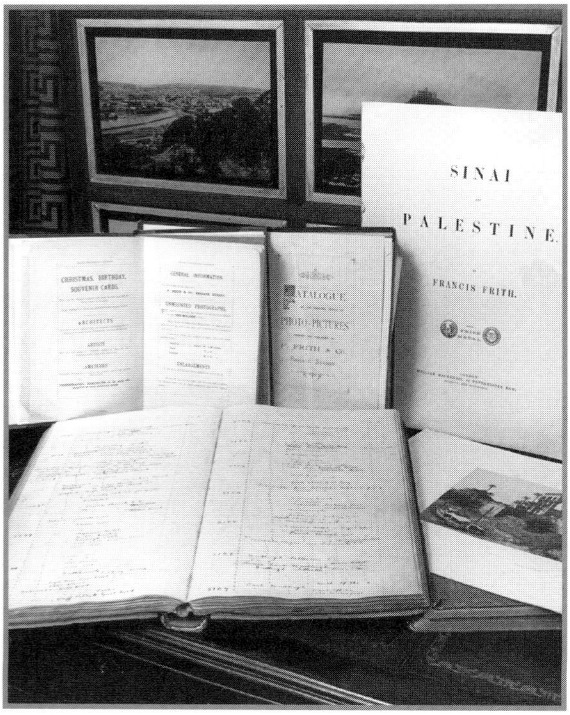

With characteristic business acumen, Francis Frith foresaw that these new tourists would enjoy having souvenirs to commemorate their days out. In 1860 he married Mary Ann Rosling and set out with the intention of photographing every city, town and village in Britain. For the next thirty years he travelled the country by train and by pony and trap, producing fine photographs of seaside resorts and beauty spots that were keenly bought by millions of Victorians. These prints were painstakingly pasted into family albums and pored over during the dark nights of winter, rekindling precious memories of summer excursions.

The Rise of Frith & Co

Frith's studio was soon supplying retail shops all over the country. To meet the demand he gathered about him a small team of photographers, and published the work of independent artist-photographers of the calibre of Roger Fenton and Francis Bedford. In order to gain some understanding of the scale of Frith's business one only has to look at the catalogue issued by Frith & Co in 1886: it runs to some 670 pages, listing not only many thousands of views of the British Isles but also many photographs of most European countries, and China, Japan, the USA and

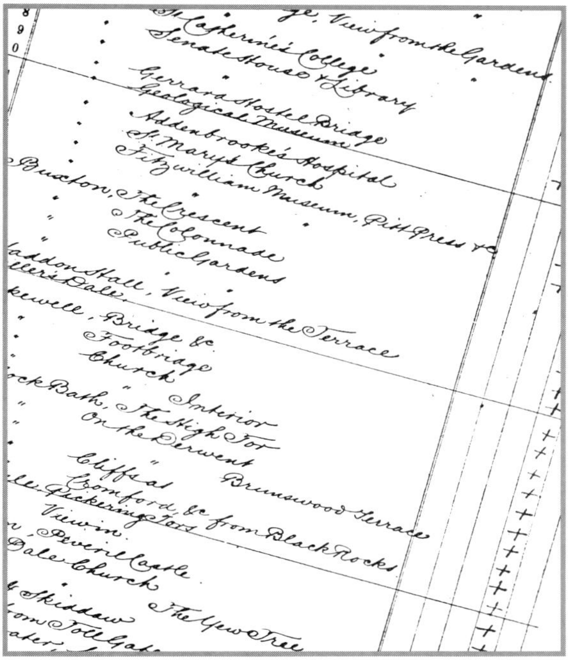
ge, View from the Gardens
St Catherine's College
Senate House & Library
Gerrard Hostel Bridge
Geological Museum
Addenbrooke's Hospital
St Mary's Church
Fitzwilliam Museum, Pitt Press &c
Buxton, The Crescent
The Colonnade
Public Gardens
Haddon Hall, View from the Terrace
Bakewell, Bridge &c.
Footbridge
Church
Matlock Bath, " Interior
The High Tor
On the Derwent
Cliffs at " Brunswood Terrace
Cromford, &c from Black Rocks
Pickering Tors
View in
Peveril Castle
Dale Church
Skiddaw The Yew Tree
From Toll Gate

Canada – note the sample page shown above from the hand-written *Frith & Co* ledgers detailing pictures taken. By 1890 Frith had created the greatest specialist photographic publishing company in the world, with over 2,000 outlets – more than the combined number that Boots and WH Smith have today! The picture on the right shows the *Frith & Co* display board at Ingleton in the Yorkshire Dales. Beautifully constructed with mahogany frame and gilt inserts, it could display up to a dozen local scenes.

Postcard Bonanza

The ever-popular holiday postcard we know today took many years to develop. In 1870 the Post Office issued the first plain cards, with a pre-printed stamp on one face. In 1894 they allowed other publishers' cards to be sent through the mail with an attached adhesive halfpenny stamp. Demand grew rapidly, and in 1895 a new size of postcard was permitted called the court card, but there was little room for illustration. In 1899, a year after Frith's death, a new card measuring 5.5 x 3.5 inches became the standard format, but it was not until 1902 that the divided back came into being, with address and message on one face and a full-size illustration on the other. *Frith & Co* were in the vanguard of postcard development, and Frith's sons Eustace and Cyril continued their father's monumental task, expanding the number of views offered to the public and recording more and more places in Britain, as the coasts and countryside were opened up to mass travel.

Francis Frith died in 1898 at his villa in Cannes, his great project still growing. The archive he created continued in business for another seventy years. By 1970 it contained over a third of a million pictures of 7,000 cities, towns and villages. The massive photographic record Frith has left to us stands as a living monument to a special and very remarkable man.

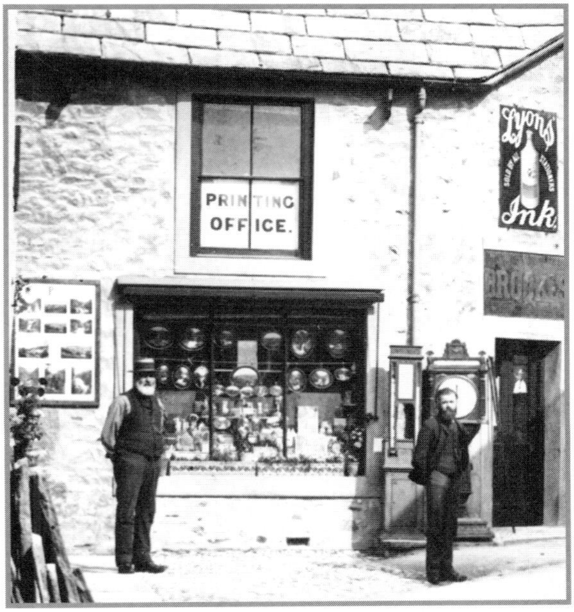

Frith's Archive: *A Unique Legacy*

FRANCIS FRITH'S legacy to us today is of immense significance and value, for the magnificent archive of evocative photographs he created provides a unique record of change in 7,000 cities, towns and villages throughout Britain over a century and more. Frith and his fellow studio photographers revisited locations many times down the years to update their views, compiling for us an enthralling and colourful pageant of British life and character.

We tend to think of Frith's sepia views of Britain as nostalgic, for most of us use them to conjure up memories of places in our own lives with which we have family associations. It often makes us forget that to Francis Frith they were records of daily life as it was actually being lived in the cities, towns and villages of his day. The Victorian age was one of great and often bewildering change for ordinary people, and though the pictures evoke an impression of slower times, life was as busy and hectic as it is today.

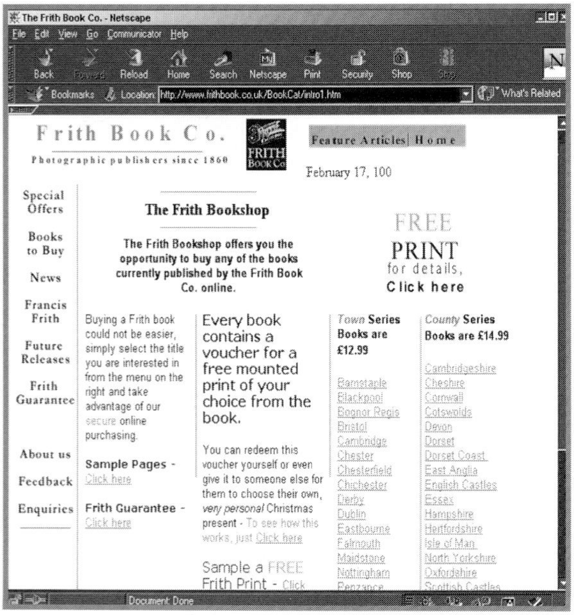

See Frith at www. frithbook.co.uk

We are fortunate that Frith was a photographer of the people, dedicated to recording the minutiae of everyday life. For it is this sheer wealth of visual data, the painstaking chronicle of changes in dress, transport, street layouts, buildings, housing, engineering and landscape that captivates us so much today. His remarkable images offer us a powerful link with the past and with the lives of our ancestors.

Today's Technology

Computers have now made it possible for Frith's many thousands of images to be accessed almost instantly. In the Frith archive today, each photograph is carefully 'digitised' then stored on a CD Rom. Frith archivists can locate a single photograph amongst thousands within seconds. Views can be catalogued and sorted under a variety of categories of place and content to the immediate benefit of researchers.

Inexpensive reference prints can be created for them at the touch of a mouse button, and a wide range of books and other printed materials assembled and published for a wider, more general readership - in the next twelve months over a hundred Frith local history titles will be published! The day-to-day workings of the archive are very different from how they were in Francis Frith's time: imagine the herculean task of sorting through eleven tons of glass negatives as Frith had to do to locate a particular sequence of pictures! Yet the archive still prides itself on maintaining the same high standards of excellence laid down by Francis Frith, including the painstaking cataloguing and indexing of every view.

It is curious to reflect on how the internet now allows researchers in America and elsewhere greater instant access to the archive than Frith himself ever enjoyed. Many thousands of individual views can be called up on screen within seconds on one of the Frith internet sites, enabling people living continents away to revisit the streets of their ancestral home town, or view places in Britain where they have enjoyed holidays. Many overseas researchers welcome the chance to view special theme selections, such as transport, sports, costume and ancient monuments.

We are certain that Francis Frith would have heartily approved of these modern developments in imaging techniques, for he himself was always working at the very limits of Victorian photographic technology.

The Value of the Archive Today

Because of the benefits brought by the computer, Frith's images are increasingly studied by social historians, by researchers into genealogy and ancestory, by architects, town planners, and by teachers and schoolchildren involved in local history projects.

In addition, the archive offers every one of us an opportunity to examine the places where we and our families have lived and worked down the years. Highly successful in Frith's own era, the archive is now, a century and more on, entering a new phase of popularity.

The Past in Tune with the Future

Historians consider the Francis Frith Collection to be of prime national importance. It is the only archive of its kind remaining in private ownership and has been valued at a million pounds. However, this figure is now rapidly increasing as digital technology enables more and more people around the world to enjoy its benefits.

Francis Frith's archive is now housed in an historic timber barn in the beautiful village of Teffont in Wiltshire. Its founder would not recognize the archive office as it is today. In place of the many thousands of dusty boxes containing glass plate negatives and an all-pervading odour of photographic chemicals, there are now ranks of computer screens. He would be amazed to watch his images travelling round the world at unimaginable speeds through network and internet lines.

The archive's future is both bright and exciting. Francis Frith, with his unshakeable belief in making photographs available to the greatest number of people, would undoubtedly approve of what is being done today with his lifetime's work. His photographs, depicting our shared past, are now bringing pleasure and enlightenment to millions around the world a century and more after his death.

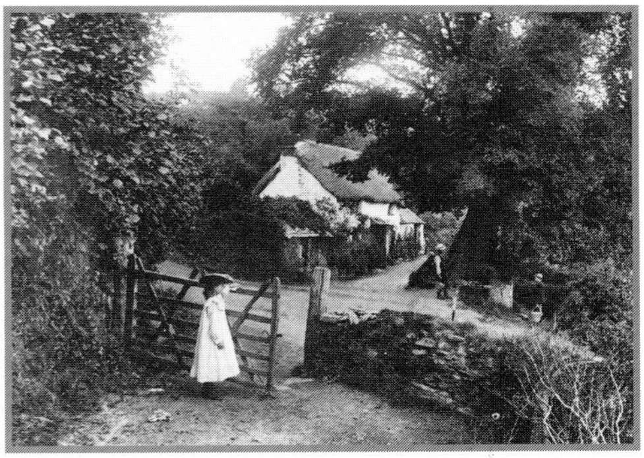

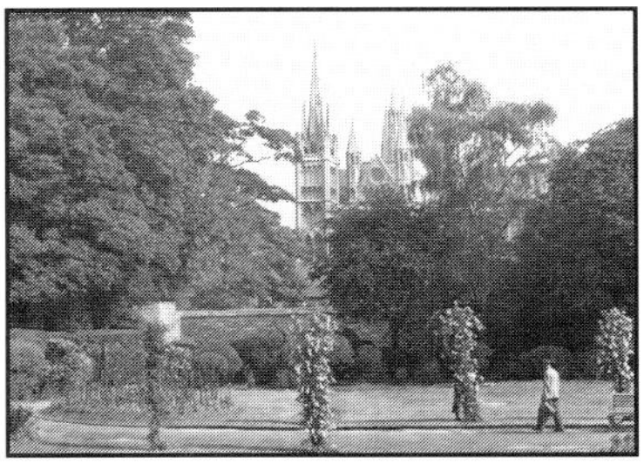

Peterborough - *An Introduction*

THE CITY OF Peterborough is situated on a limestone promontory on the River Nene on the northern boundary of Northamptonshire where East Anglia meets the East Midlands, 75 miles north of London; it has a fascinating history, and has prospered from the produce of fields, fen and forest.

For many years the centre of the city was almost overwhelmed by the great bulk of St Peter's cathedral, a magnificent example of Norman and Early English architecture, with additions built in later years. The illustrious building has the distinction of having once had two queens, Catherine of Aragon and Mary Queen of Scots, buried beneath its paving; both were later removed to Westminster Abbey. Robert Scarlett, better known by his nickname 'old Scarlett', which suited his grim and stocky appearance, was the local man who buried them both.

Long before that period of massive upheaval in English history, the Romans built a town here called Durobrivae and a 27-acre fortress under what is now Thorpe Wood golf course; excavation even revealed evidence of prehistoric settlement here from 3, 500 BC. The Saxons called the town Medeshamstede - the name means 'settlement in the meadow'. Northamptonshire belonged to the Midland kingdom of Mercia when the pagan King

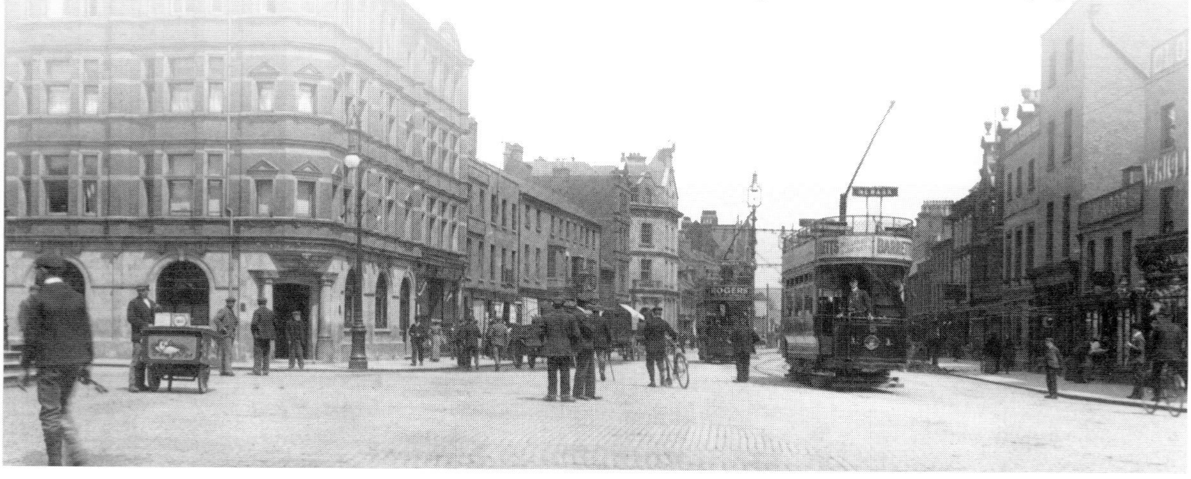

Penda was killed fighting the Northumbrians in 654. His son and successor was a Christian, who established a monastery at Medeshamstede dedicated to St Peter; Saxulf became the first abbot in 675.

There is nowadays debate about the extent of violence from the Danish Viking invasions. Their earliest incursions during the 9th century left evidence that East Anglia was harshly treated. The monastery was laid waste, and the Bishop of Leicester fled to Dorchester. Alfred's treaty of Wedmore in 878 contained the Danes, and by the 10th century Viking forces were waning. Signs of these times remain in many Danish local place-names north of the Welland. Though famed for fighting , the Vikings were a trading people; as settlers, they had helped to boost the local economy by the time that Edward the elder's son Aethelstan finally defeated Danelaw.

Alas, the Danes obliterated most evidence of the early monastery. St Aethelwold, Bishop of Winchester, revived the monasteries: apparently he followed a vision calling him to Oundle, where he found ruins and repaired them. Going on to Medeshamstede, he built a large new house, enclosing it with strong walls and calling it a burgh; eventually the saint's name was added to create Peter Burgh, which was later modified to Peterborough.

The Normans invaded a land governed under a system of Hundreds and Hundred Courts. Seeking improvements, they began with a little stock-taking, the Domesday survey. Abbot Leofric was close to King Harold, and died with him at Hastings. Turold, his Norman successor at Peterborough, was well-equipped as a warrior to deal with Hereward the Wake and his outlaws, who came to the city to burn it and steal treasure. The Normans needed an iron hand to defend their position nationally. Fire destroyed the Abbey again in 1116; the core of the present cathedral was built on the site as an abbey church between 1118 and 1258. The nave was built from local Barnack stone with large piers and eleven bays. The town grew as a settlement outside the abbey gates, and William added an earth and timber castle with provision for 60 knights. Feudalism was operating with ruthless efficiency: land values rose steadily, with Northamptonshire among the most prosperous areas.

The Black Death took its toll in 1349, but in the long term this promoted farming efficiency. Over-cropping and overpopulation had created crop failure, famines and epidemics. The Fens attracted much of the region's population, and the roads were busy with traders and dealers.

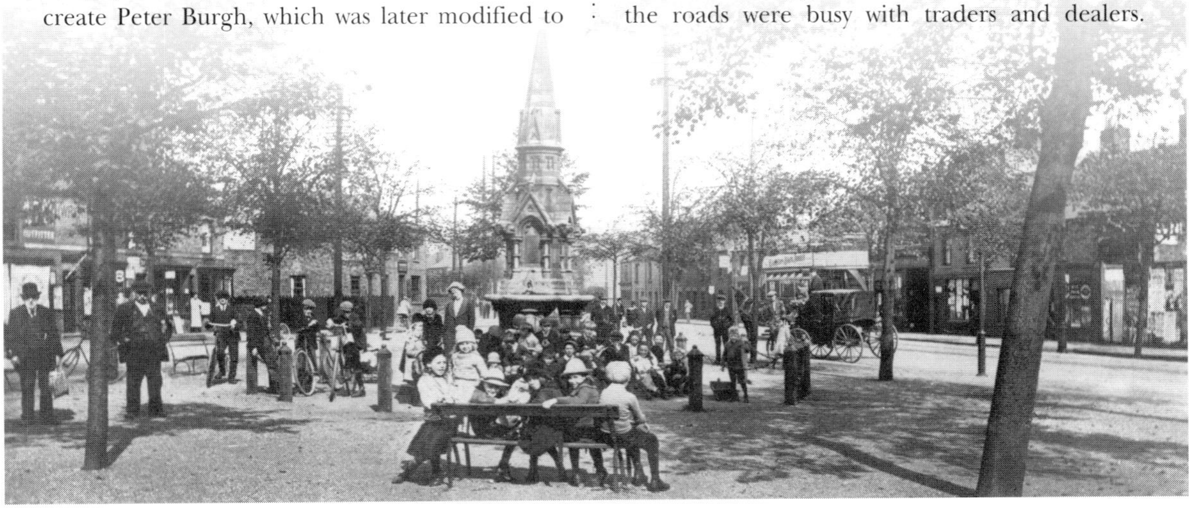

Religious houses tapped directly into this prosperity; Peterborough took some of the richest pickings. When Henry VIII passed the Act of Supremacy in 1534, he chose to dissolve nunneries and monasteries, pocketing a fortune. His actions originated from his need to divorce, which forced him to abandon the Catholic church. Henry knew Peterborough from his childhood; he had visited his grandmother Lady Beaufort there. He had also shown a strong interest in ecclesiastical matters since his early training for the priesthood had been cut short by his brother's death. Aiming to increase his bishoprics, Henry made the Abbey a college for priests. Removing Northampton and Rutland from the medieval see of Lincoln in 1541, he made Peterborough the centre of his new diocese.

Relative peace ensued until the English Civil War. East Anglia harboured the Parliamentarians, who were protecting the supply routes from London. Their troops showed no respect for a grand cathedral, and desecrated it with enthusiasm. The locals were pleased to see a monarch restored in 1660; they added an upper floor to their old town hall in honour of the event in 1671. An Act of Uniformity in 1662 attempted to impose religious conformity, and so boosted dissent. In 1695 Bishop White of Peterborough refused to accept William and Mary as monarchs, and lost his living. Unbridled Protestantism and its work ethic were to inspire the future.

Peterborough's population reached 3000 by 1790, though the traditional woolcombing industry was in decline. Napoleon was the national enemy, with French prisoners of war coming by boat along the Nene and being

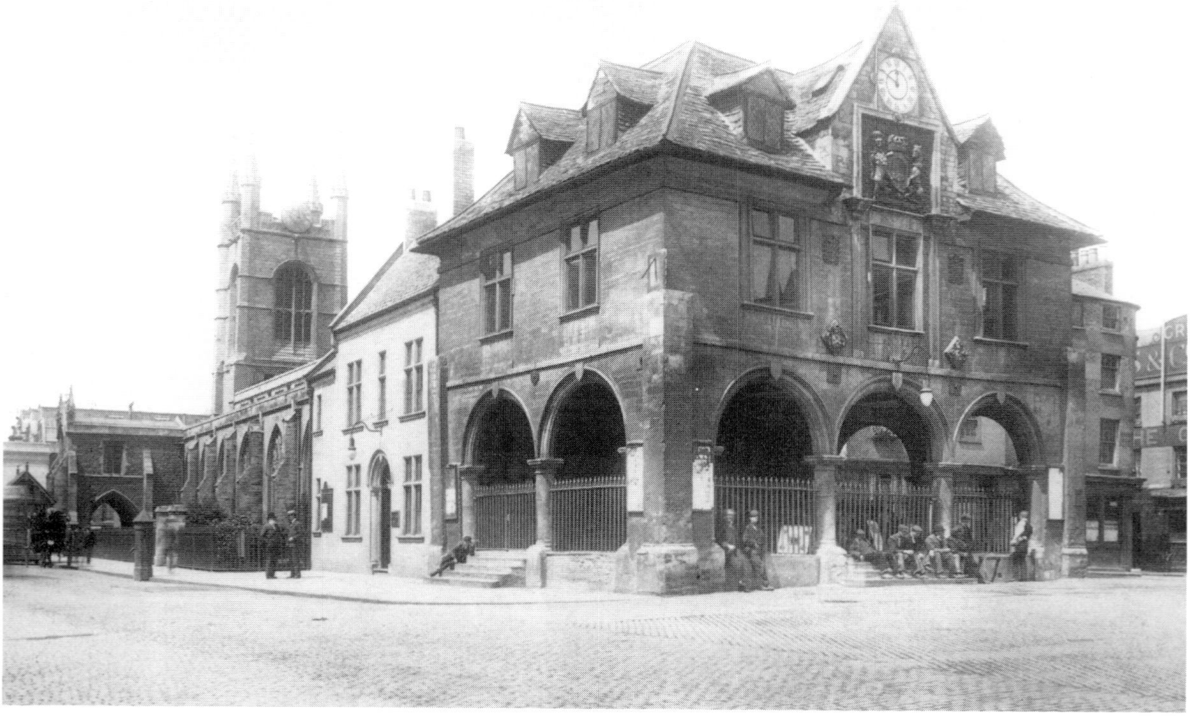

The Town Hall and the Church 1904 51546

marched to a camp at Norman Cross. By 1816 the camp had outgrown the city - its population reached 10,000. The prisoners amused themselves by carving model ships from meat bones and selling them locally.

By this time the city had Improvement Commissioners, but they could not meet the people's growing needs. More money was needed. The first police force in 1874 comprised a Chief Constable, 3 sergeants and 14 men. It was plagued with drunkenness. Streets were lit by oil lamps, and toll bars were erected across city entrances. Farm and fair traffic, along with local traffic, was exempt. However, progress was slow, because politics were corrupt. The powerful Fitzwilliams were adept at buying votes. Local government reforms and secret ballots toward the end of the 19th century brought democracy a little closer. The Parliamentary Boundary Commission of 1874 included parts of Fletton and Woodston, which were integral to the local economy. Earl Fitzwilliam chaired a meeting to consider building a railway from Blisworth and Northampton to Peterborough. Parliamentary approval was gained in July 1843, and Peterborough became an important junction. Railways encouraged the local brick-making industry and the Fletton revolution.

The Fletton process was stimulated by the rapid growth of Peterborough - the population increased from 17,429 in 1871 to 30,000 in 1898. It originated in 1881 following the auction of Fletton Lodge Estate, which was sold as land with brick-making potential. The Fletton brick was born when one of the new brickmakers leasing part of the estate discarded the surface or callow clay to obtain the deeper shaley blue Oxford clay. Many more brickmakers soon discovered this material's amazing potential. Being carboniferous, it burned with only a little outside help from coal dust (called smudge). The clay lay in deep uniform good-quality strata, so excavation was relatively easy, though dangerous. The discovery sparked something like a gold rush. Crucial among the pioneers were Hempsted Bros, who leased 40 acres of the old estate at Fletton. With an established background in engineering, they had the skills to mechanise an old craft industry. Dry clay was taken to the works, where it was ground to a powder and made into bricks using presses which applied extreme pressure from four different directions. Hence, Fletton bricks under London Brick Company manufacture were trademarked 'Phorpres'.

Presses capable of making 3000 bricks in ten hours were available by 1911. Arthur Werner Itter was a Fletton pioneer at his Saxon works near

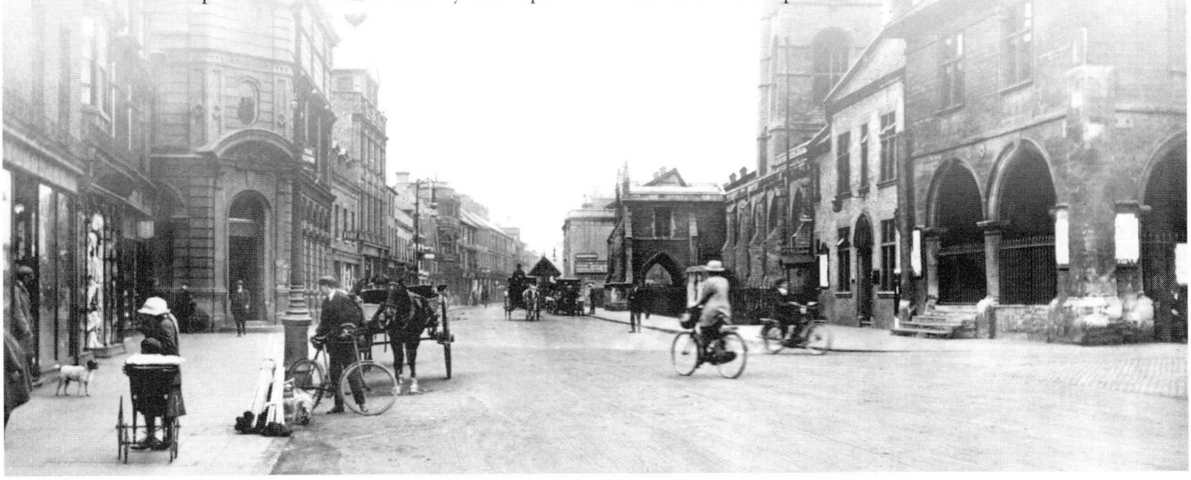

Peterborough. The bricks were fired (literally burned) in the new continuous Hoffman kilns. Heat from burning bricks in one chamber was channelled to the next, drying the bricks stacked there, thus making them easy to fire. Fire went around all the chambers, with various ones being filled, burnt or emptied. A lot of bricks had to be sold to meet the capital costs of keeping the kilns burning and digging out the huge pits or knot holes to provide the clay. J C Hill was another local pioneer; eventually, they and Hempsted Bros became part of the London Brick Company, following a series of cartels and mergers to maintain prices and reduce competition. Conventional brick-making was reduced to a rump, even though it might claim to be a better-quality hand-crafted product.

The modern London Brick Company derived its name from supplying the capital's increasing needs. The rail link was crucial, although by the 1930s the company had built up a fleet of delivery lorries which were a familiar sight in the area. By 1923, all the major Peterborough district brick yards, including Warboys and nine small independents, had been engulfed. The Second World War boosted London's brick demands for shelters and repairs, making the railways even busier.

Engineers were a vital ingredient of the modern brick industry, and the city was rich in them owing to the challenges of local agriculture. Frank Perkins was the son of a local agricultural engineer, who worked for the family firm of Barford and Perkins, helping to mechanise local farmers. Frank was surplus to requirements during the 1930s depression, and founded his own business developing high-quality diesel engines. His four circle badge became an internationally famous symbol of excellence, though early days were a struggle. A contract to provide engines for the Commer Superpoise kept his business safe. Engineering also flourished with the railways, though this industry was noted for unrest during the inter-war years.

The Second World War was perhaps Peterborough's biggest upheaval, with many

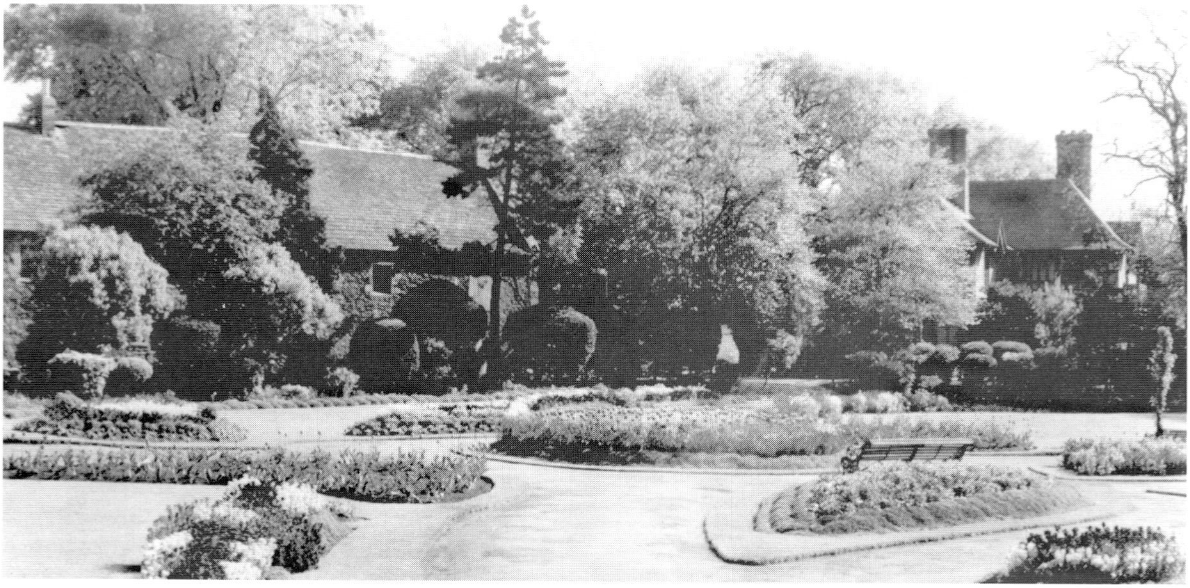

Peterborough, Bishop's Road Gardens c1955 P47002

newcomers to the city. Mass Observation surveys recorded that local folk were hostile to outsiders. In 1943 they reported that 'there was great resentment to American troops stationed locally'. Interestingly enough, it seems that this view was not widely shared by young local females! The survey supposed that the problem was due to the many new industries, conflict between old and new and pressure on billets and shopping. Apparently at that time 'it simply isn't fit for a decent girl to walk through the streets at night now'.

Since those good old days, much has been done to enhance the city's streets. As H F Tebbs noted in his erudite study, Peterborough was the first city to experience planned growth. Many farm workers had to leave the fens during the turn of the 19th century depression, when the Ministry of Agriculture declared that British farming was dead and fit for burial. Fortunately, railways and brick-making were there to take up the slack. During the mid 1960s, the South-East Economic Planning Council planned four major swathes of development stretching away from London: the plan aimed to make great use of motorways and existing main rail lines up to 1975, and also to accommodate growth away from London and to protect the countryside. This was the age of Milton Keynes and expanding Northampton. During these years of change, Peterborough would get caught up in the process; it experienced unprecedented growth, using all the know-how that modern planners, engineers and builders had to offer. Though the results could not please everyone, Peterborough had to move with the times, and will continue to do so.

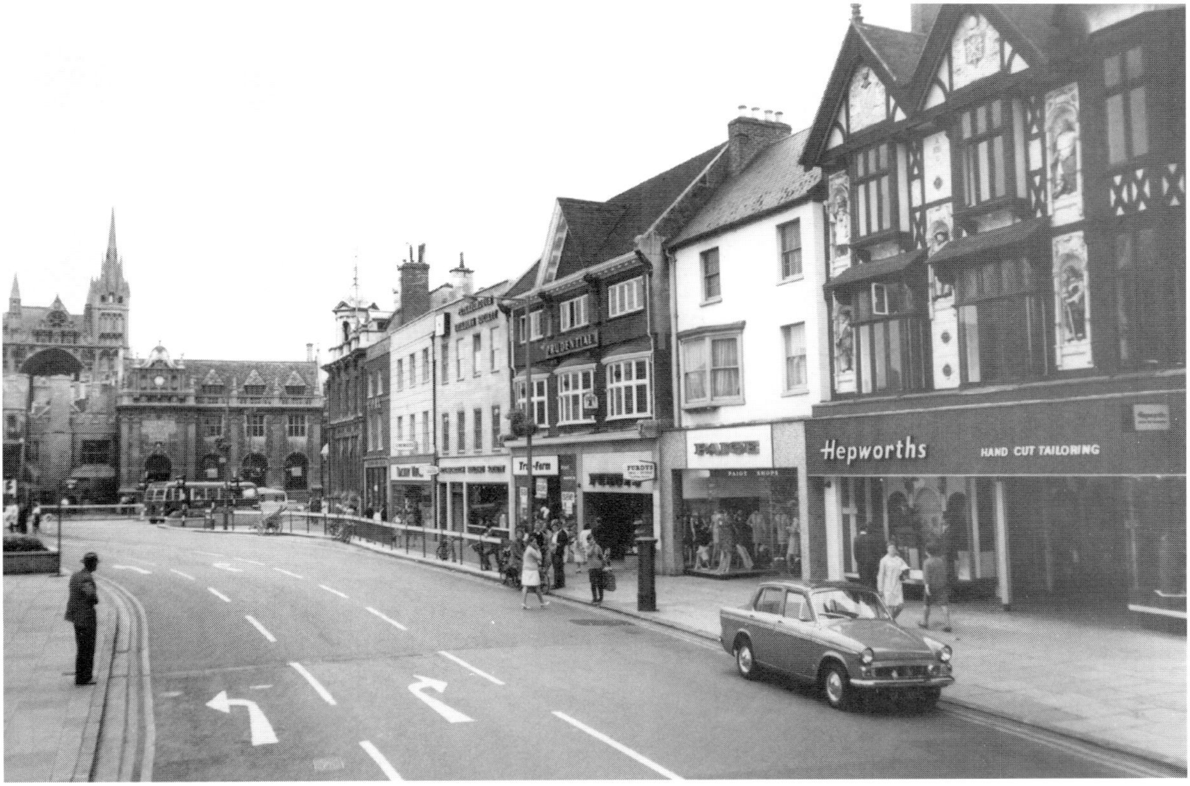

Church Street and The Square c1965 P47079

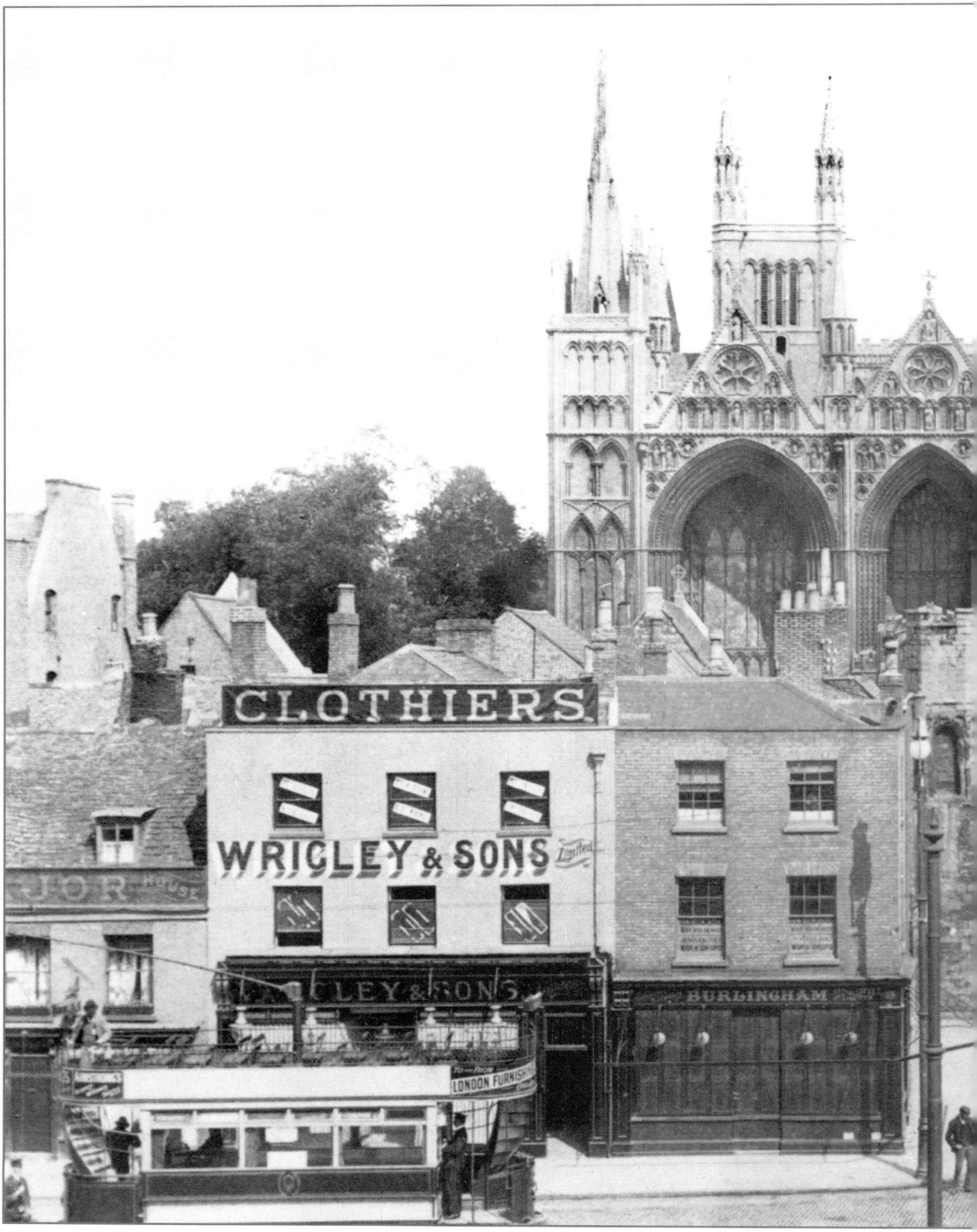
CLOTHIERS
WRIGLEY & SONS
Limited
BURLINGHAM
LONDON FURNISHING

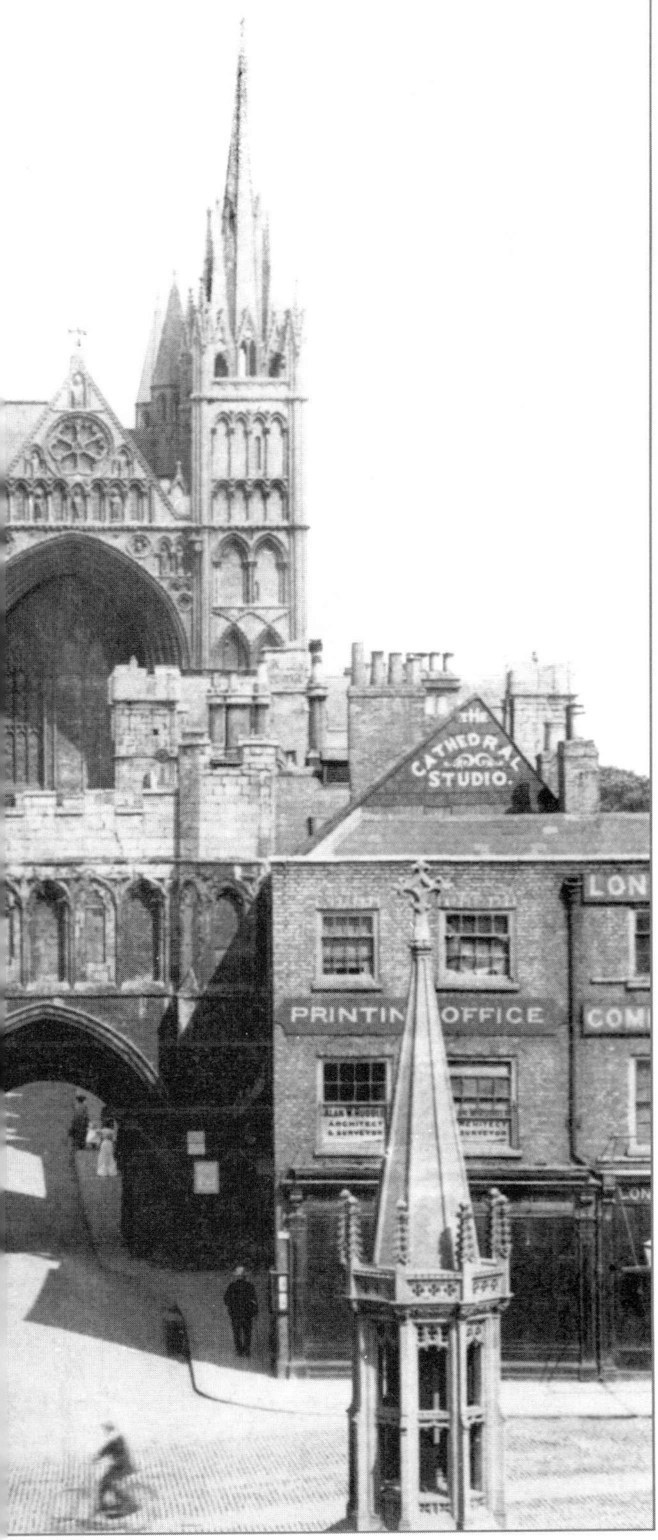

City Life

Peterborough has known all the trappings of market town prosperity, with fairs and sales providing all necessities and more. Everyday life has been punctuated by periods of upheaval, resulting in gradual or sudden, often violent, change. The Vikings struck fiercely at times, but they brought trade also. Plague and other epidemics thrived on poverty and ignorance; the solutions were waiting, for doors were to open toward greater enlightenment - the Reformation, the Napoleonic Wars, the Industrial and Agrarian Revolutions, the reforming of the franchise and two World Wars forced the way to many such doors. After each upheaval, life was never quite the same. If progress is measured by the ability to feed more people and to keep more people alive, then there has been much of it. But more people and their needs create more scope for conflict. People want to have a sense of belonging, and ►

The Market Place and the Cathedral 1904 51544
The Cathedral and the shops are viewed from St John's Church, across Broad Bridge Street. St Nicholas's Gateway and the west front of the Cathedral are shown in fine detail. All the shops are of a practical variety, and two boast a London link. Gates' memorial peeps up into the foreground, and we can see one of the new Peterborough Electric Traction Company's 12 trams.

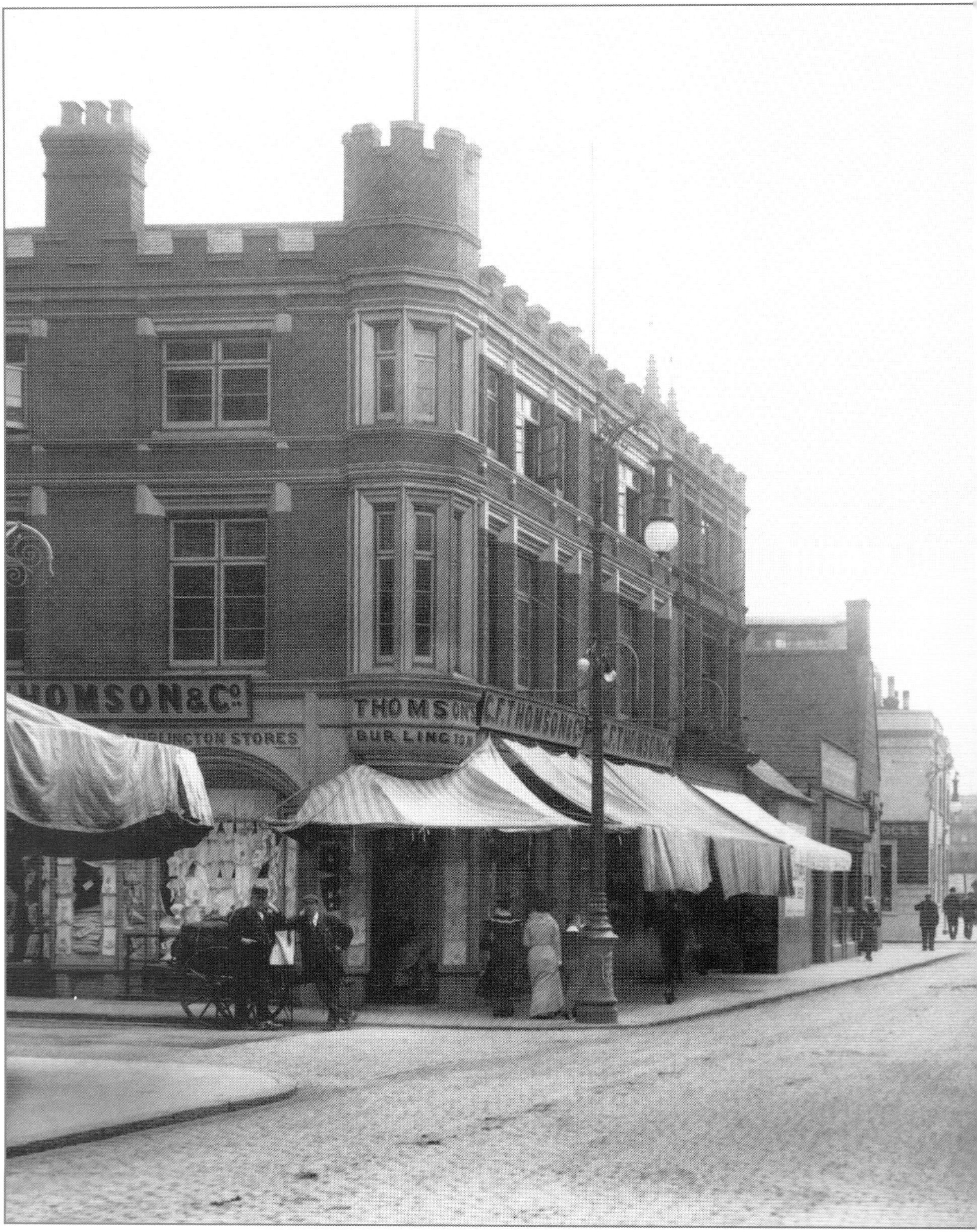
THOMSON & Co
BURLINGTON STORES
THOMSON'S
BURLINGTON
C.F. THOMSON & Co
C.F. THOMSON & Co

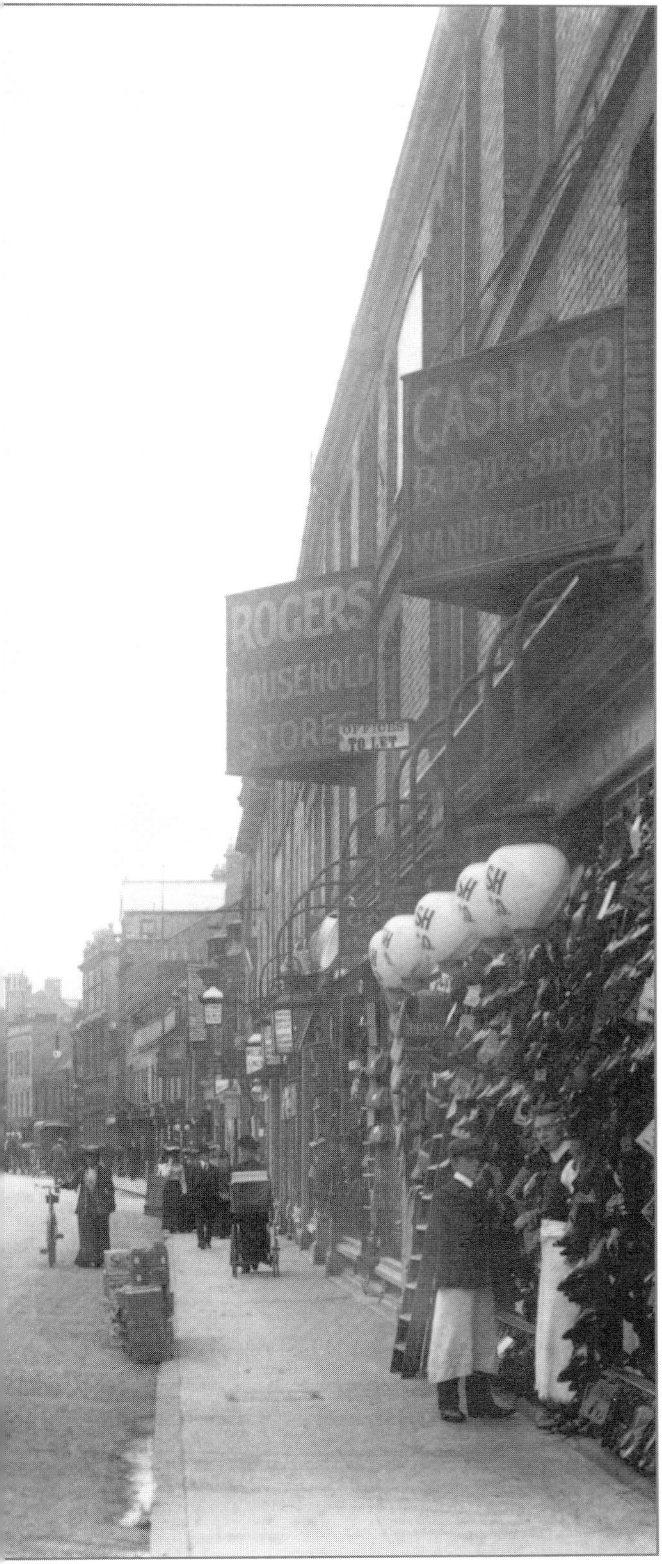

they have become accustomed to improved working conditions and better entertainment. Over the years, the city burghers, administrators and MPs did their best to create what we have today. But politics is the art of the possible, and perfection is currently impossible.

The planners have done a good job by retaining the historic atmosphere of the centre while almost hiding the Queensgate shopping complex. They have tackled the problem of getting ever more cars in and out, and have provided parking in a multi-storey that has areas named after people with local associations like Frederick Royce (an apprentice at the Great Northern Railway), Cavell and Perkins. All this is far removed from Medeshamstede and the days when freedom was something that most dare not contemplate. When Francis Frith first came this way, he photographed streets that his crisp glass plate images easily romanticised; but behind those walls was a life of hard toil for most folk. Look carefully at the stiff and formal poses and postures of street life in the early pictures, and contrast them with the more relaxed and bustling figures of the 1960s.

Cowgate 1904 51559

In Peterborough's case, the term gate derives from the Danish 'gata' meaning road. The large turreted building on the left was Cornelius Fortune Thomson's Burlington Stores. Opposite, Cash and Co display an array of footwear, undoubtedly from thriving Northamptonshire shoemakers.

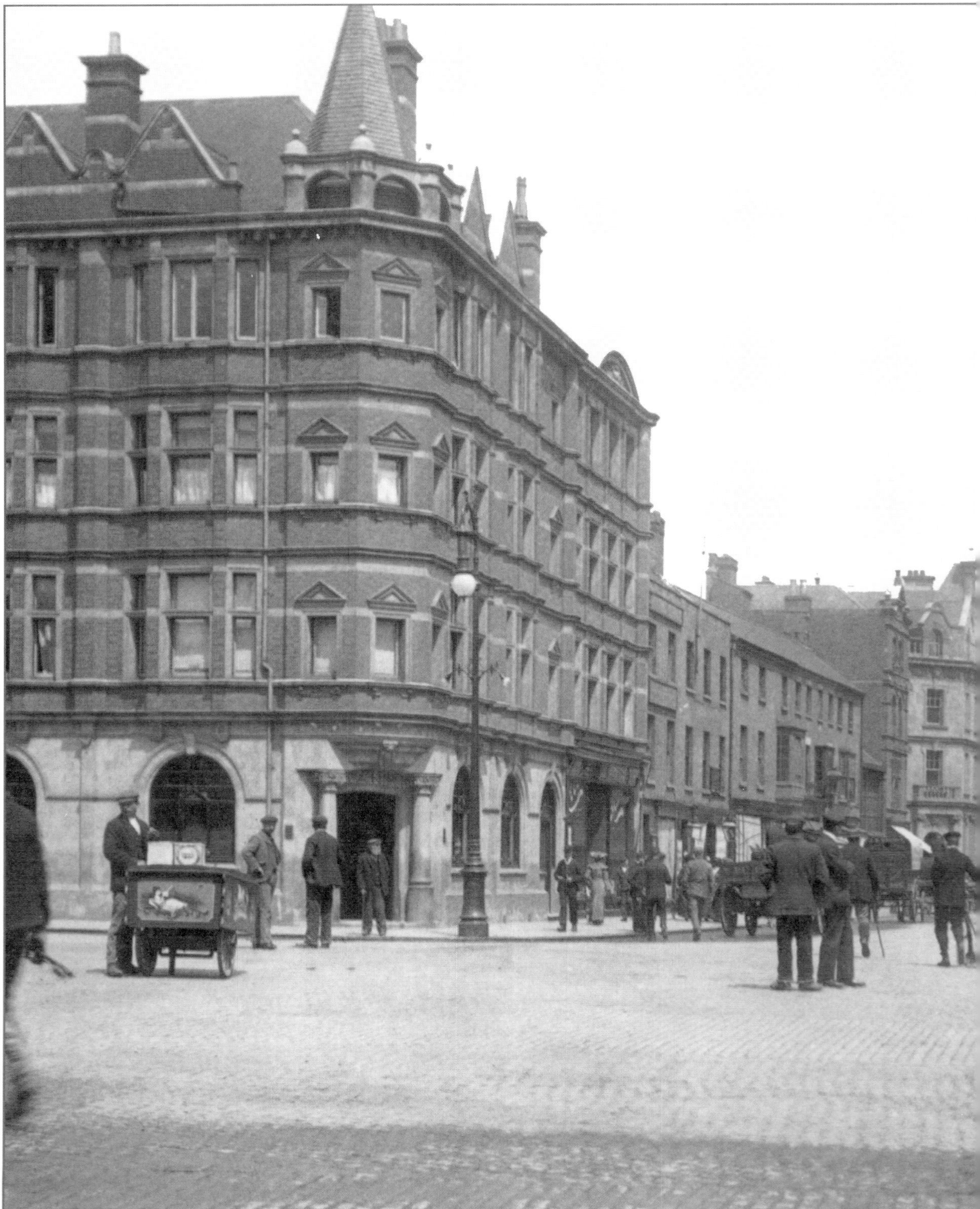

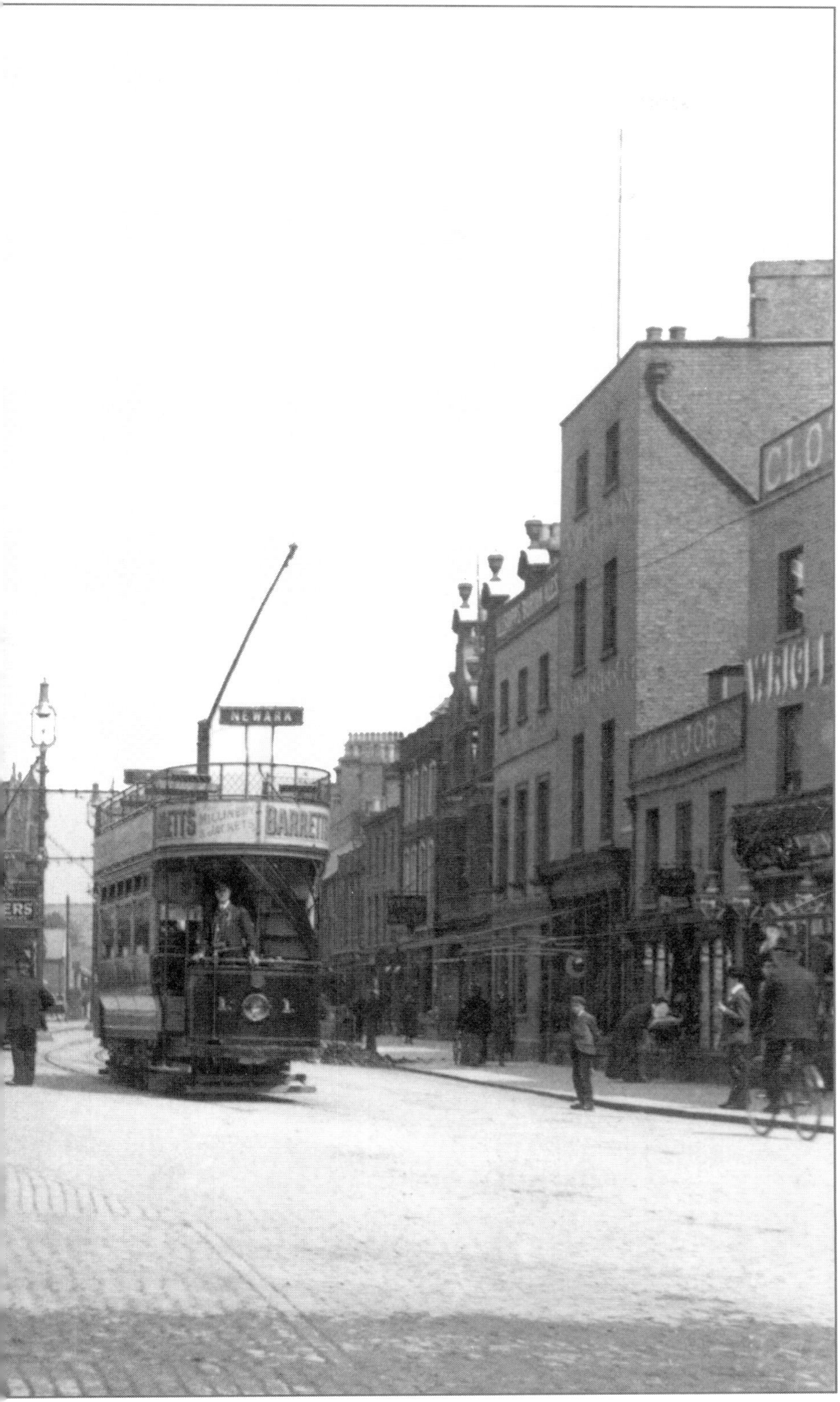

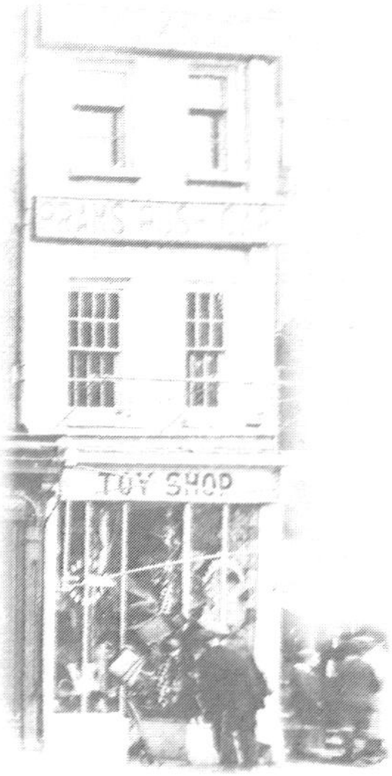

Narrow Street 1919 69094

Long Causeway, 1904
51548
This photograph was taken from in front of the cathedral. The large building on the left housed the department store of R J Glass, where shop girls worked long hours for 4s 10d for a week's work in the 1930s. In this scene, tram car number one, with its imperious conductor, is resplendent in Corporation livery as it waits at the terminus.

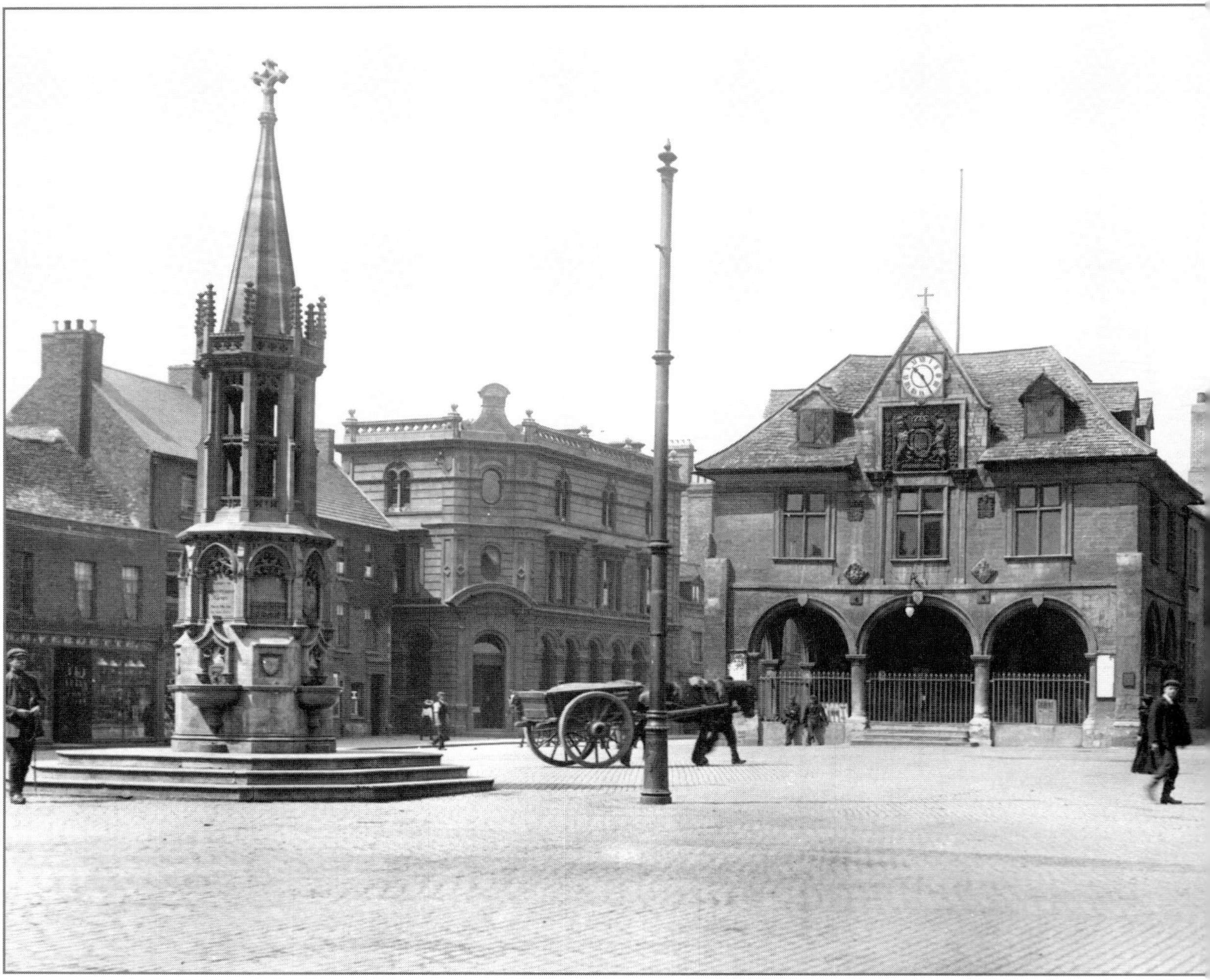

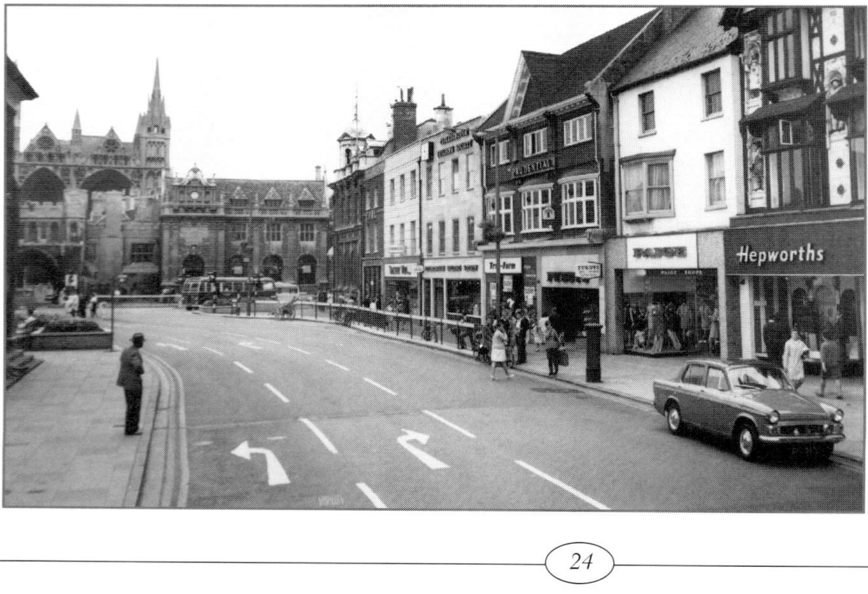

Church Street c1965

P47079

Here we see a sedate shopping scene. The shop fronts are alluring, but not brash. The illegally-parked and shining Hillman Minx is a forerunner of the age of mass motoring, which will soon overwhelm the city's streets.

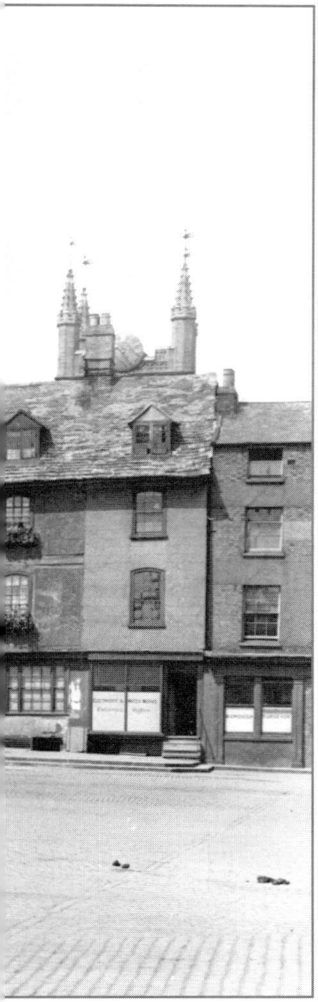

◄ **Market Place 1904** 51545
The Guildhall is in the centre, and the Gates Memorial drinking fountain to the left. The memorial was given by the chief magistrate and the widow of the first mayor (under the 1874 Charter), Pearson Gates. The tall building behind it was demolished to accommodate a half-timbered building for the new Boots chemist in 1911. The tall lean rickety Dickensian building in front of the church housed the electricity and waterworks offices.

▼ **Laurel Court 1904** 51555
Here Miss Gibson followed the Bishop's suggestion to open a school for high-class girls, and here Nurse Edith Cavell taught. The lawns would either have been mown by a pony-pulled mower (the pony wore little leather boots to protect the grass) or one of Ransomes new petrol mowers - Ransomes were a fairly local firm based at Ipswich.

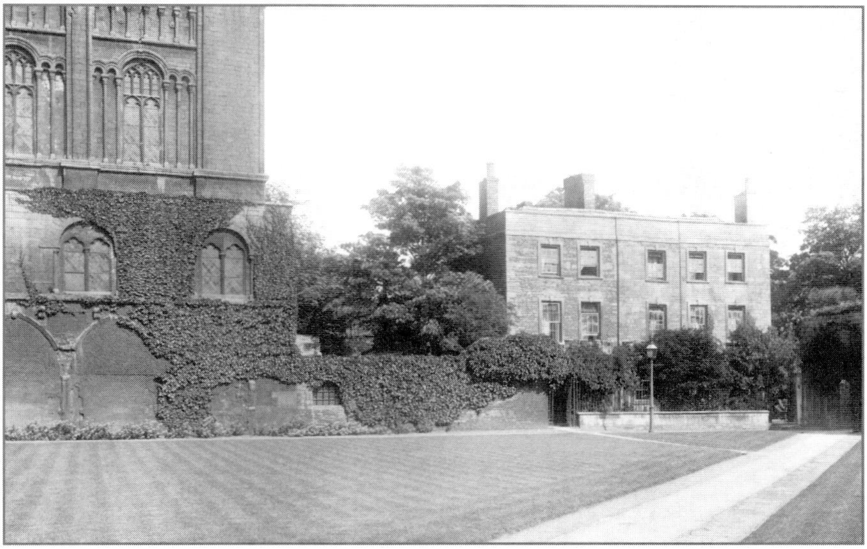

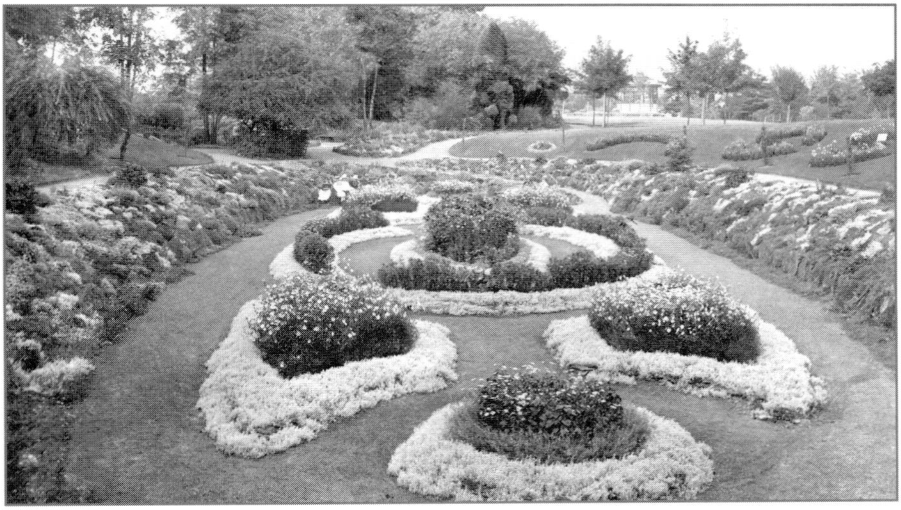

◄ **The Park 1919** 69101
Where have all the flowers gone? They are here in the park, and a fitting reminder of all the men lost during the First World War, which ended less than a year before this picture was taken. Nurse Edith Cavell had also gone, condemned to death by firing squad for helping prisoners escape; she was shot point blank by an officer because the squad faltered.

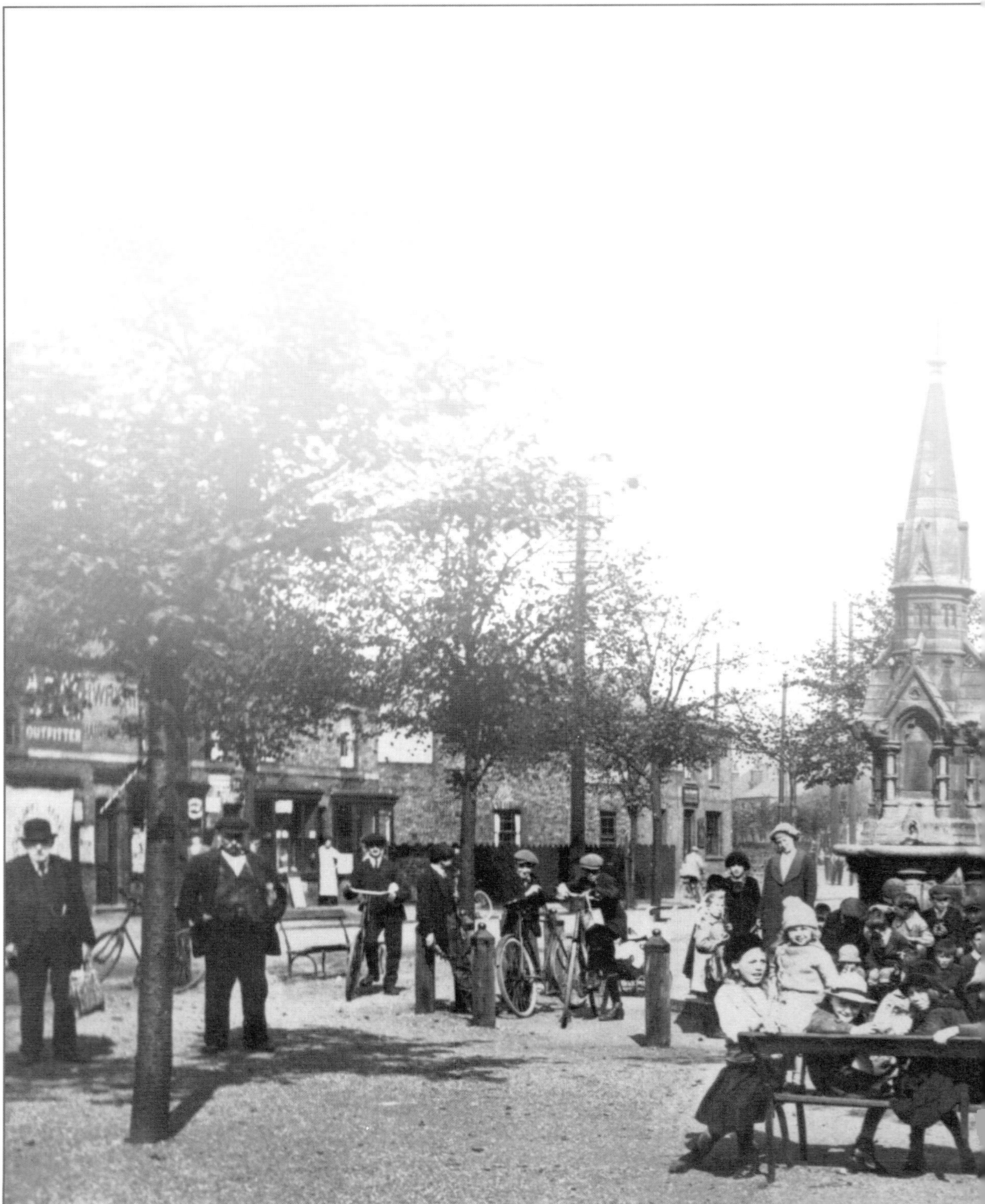
OUTFITTER

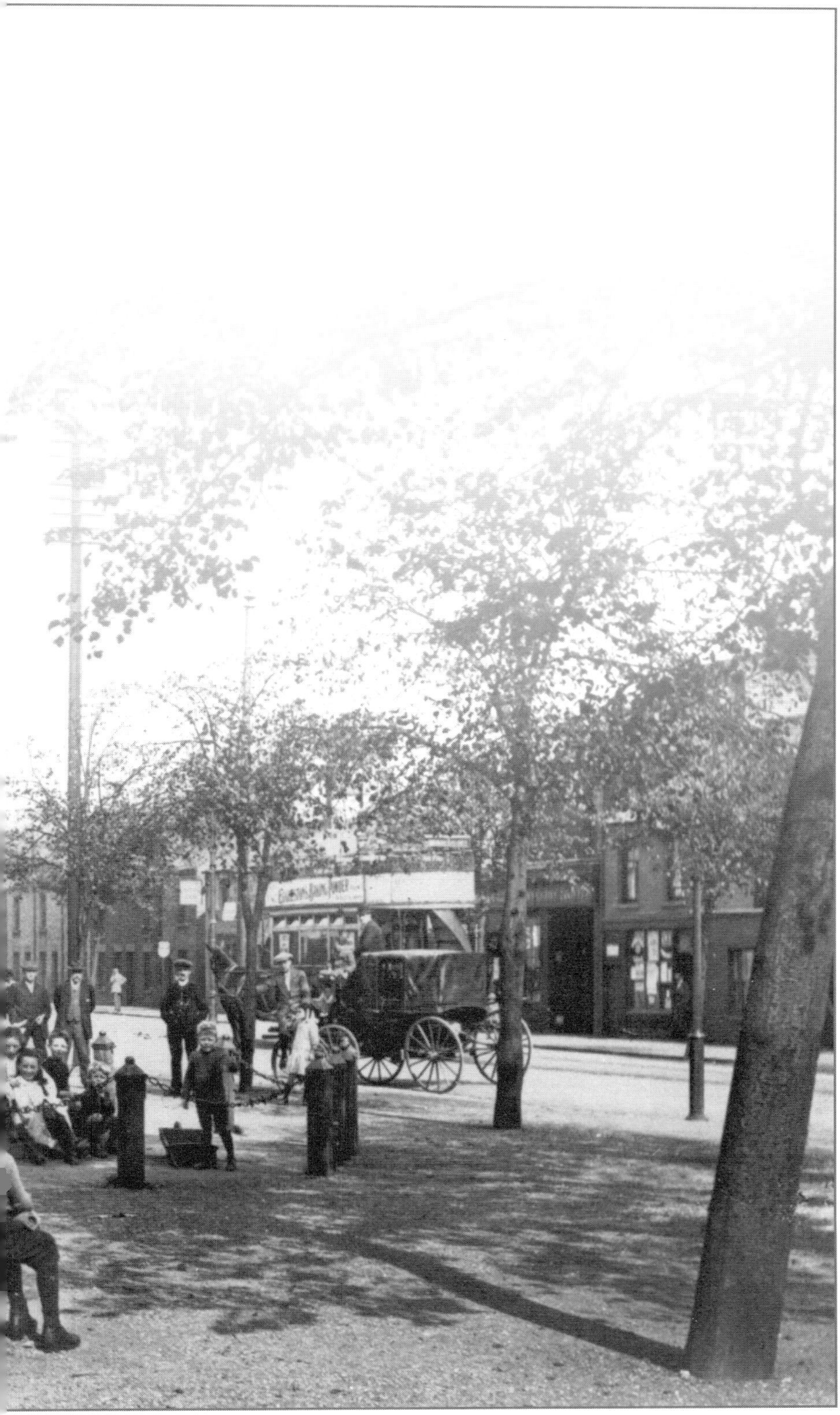

The Fountain 1919
69100
This fountain at New England was donated by the vicar, the Rev C R Ball, and his sisters as a memorial to their parents; it was unveiled on 6 November 1884. It is no longer the popular meeting place we see here, when a varied group posed for Francis Frith's camera. This was a time when a bicycle was more of a luxury than today's cars.

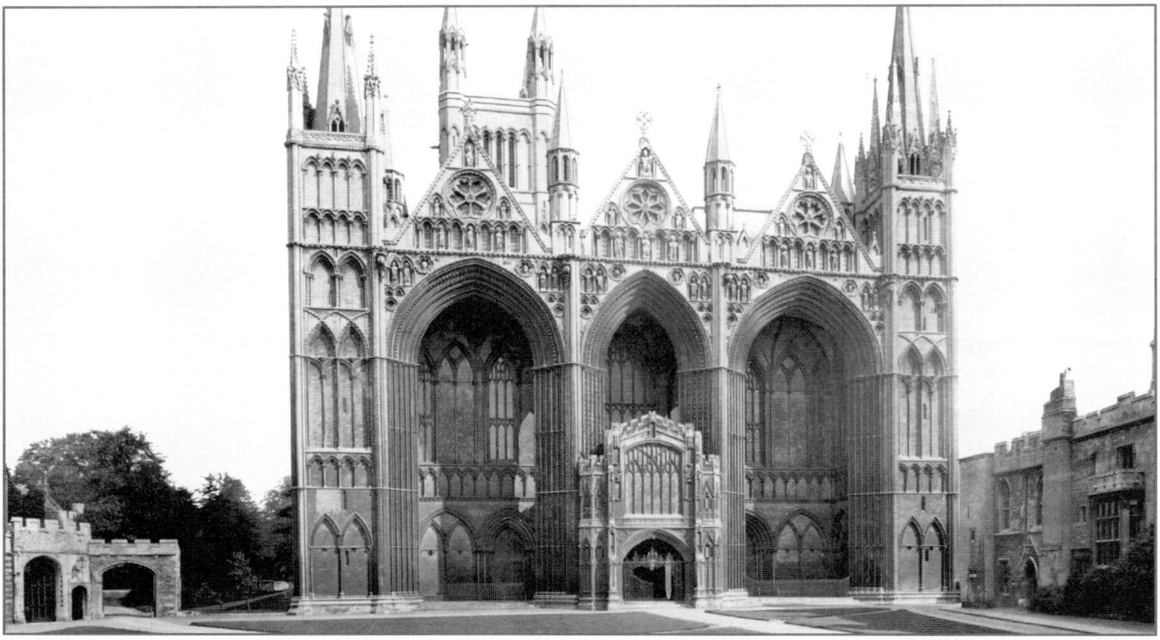

The Cathedral 1919 69082
At this time, Peterborough's people were looking hopefully toward peace after a brutal war whose only consolation had been that God was supposed to be on our side. If these great walls had ears, they had undoubtedly heard it all before.

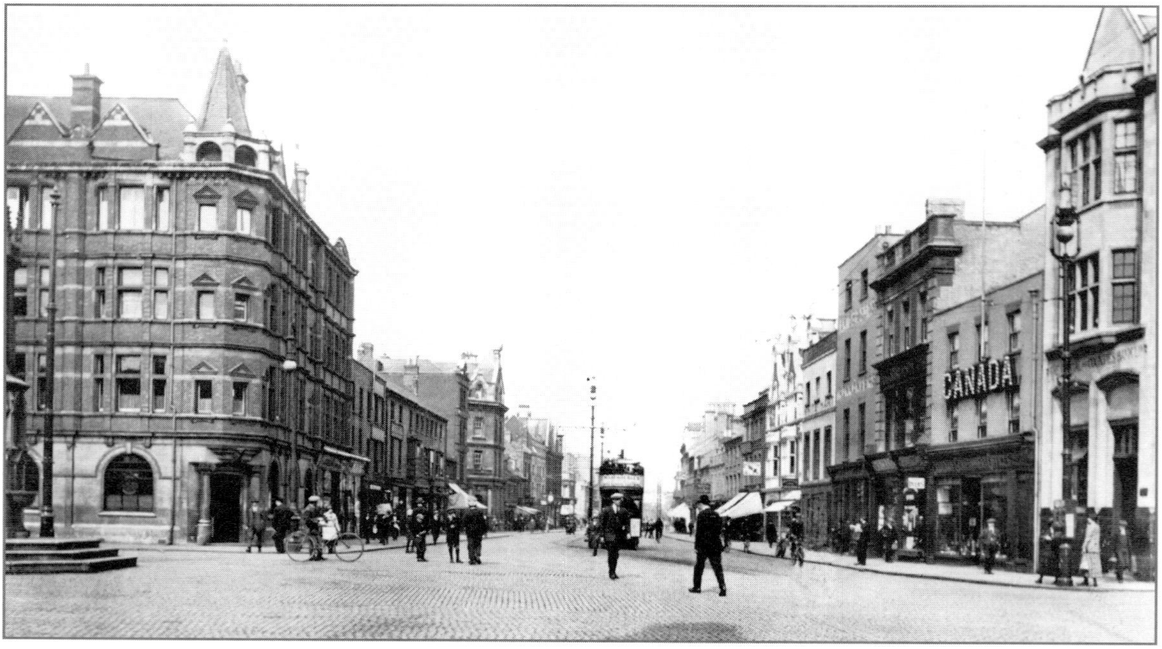

Long Causeway 1919 69095
This view shows a broad expanse of cobbles. R J Glass's sombre edifice, left, dominates the building line, so much of which has made way for today's modern shopping facilities. Opposite, the Canadian Government offices remind us that at this time there was still something of an empire, and opportunities in wide open spaces abroad.

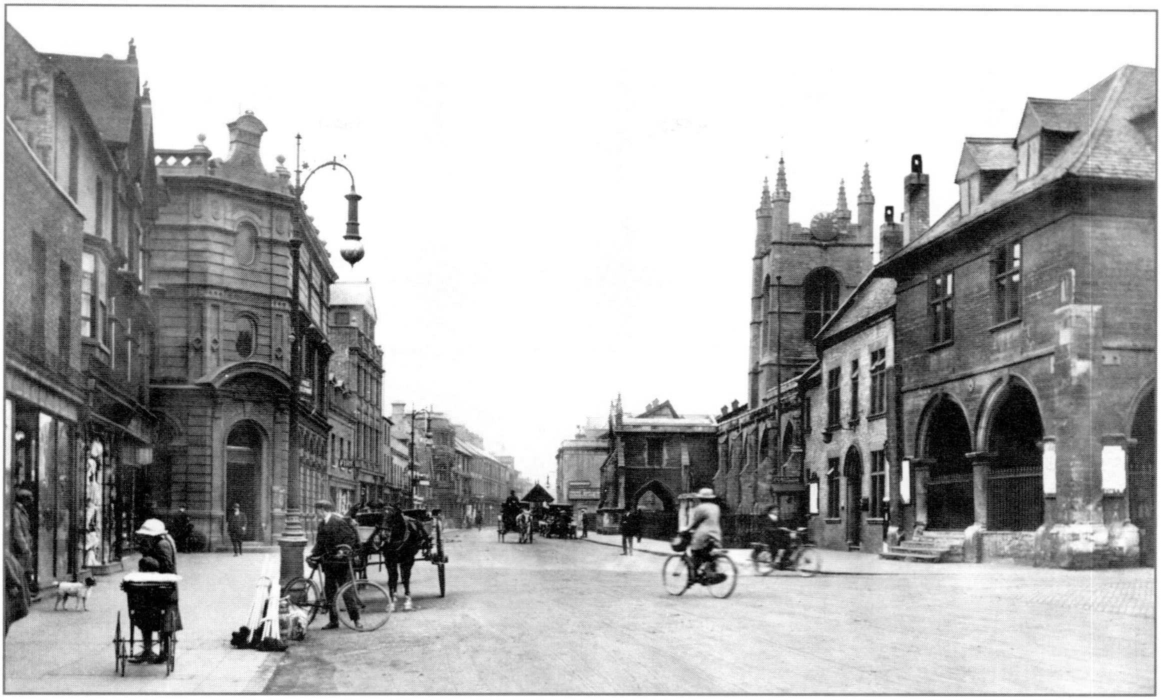

Church Street 1919 69092
Church Street, its name linked to the Parish Church of St John the Baptist, looks lively here, mixing horse power old and new and pedals too! Such elegance, even in the street lamps and the girl's perambulator, is not seen today. These people are hoping for a brighter future, but as Ruby Hill recalls: 'It wasn't long before we saw men standing in Peterborough's streets , unemployed and diving for dog ends desperate for a smoke'.

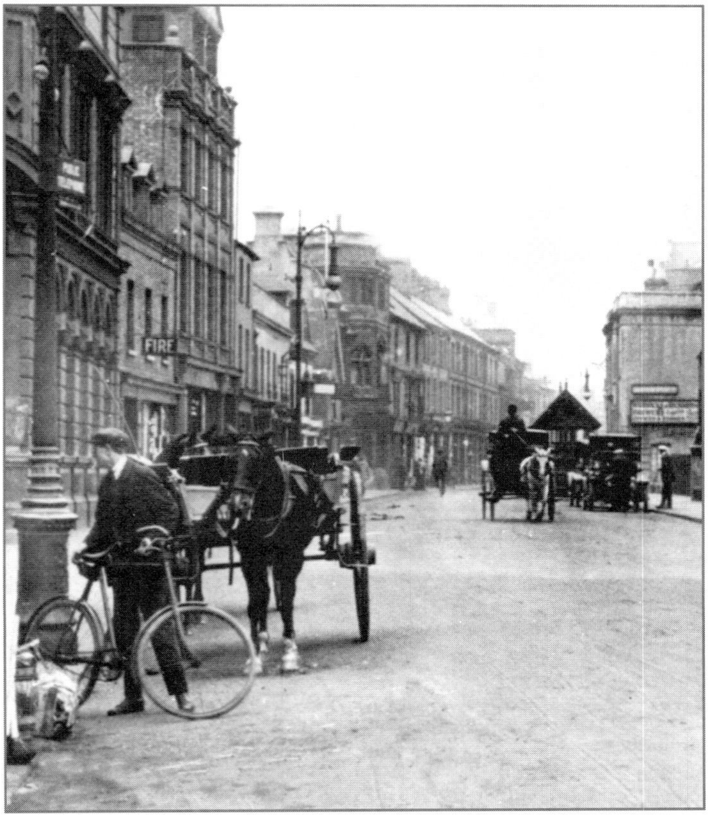

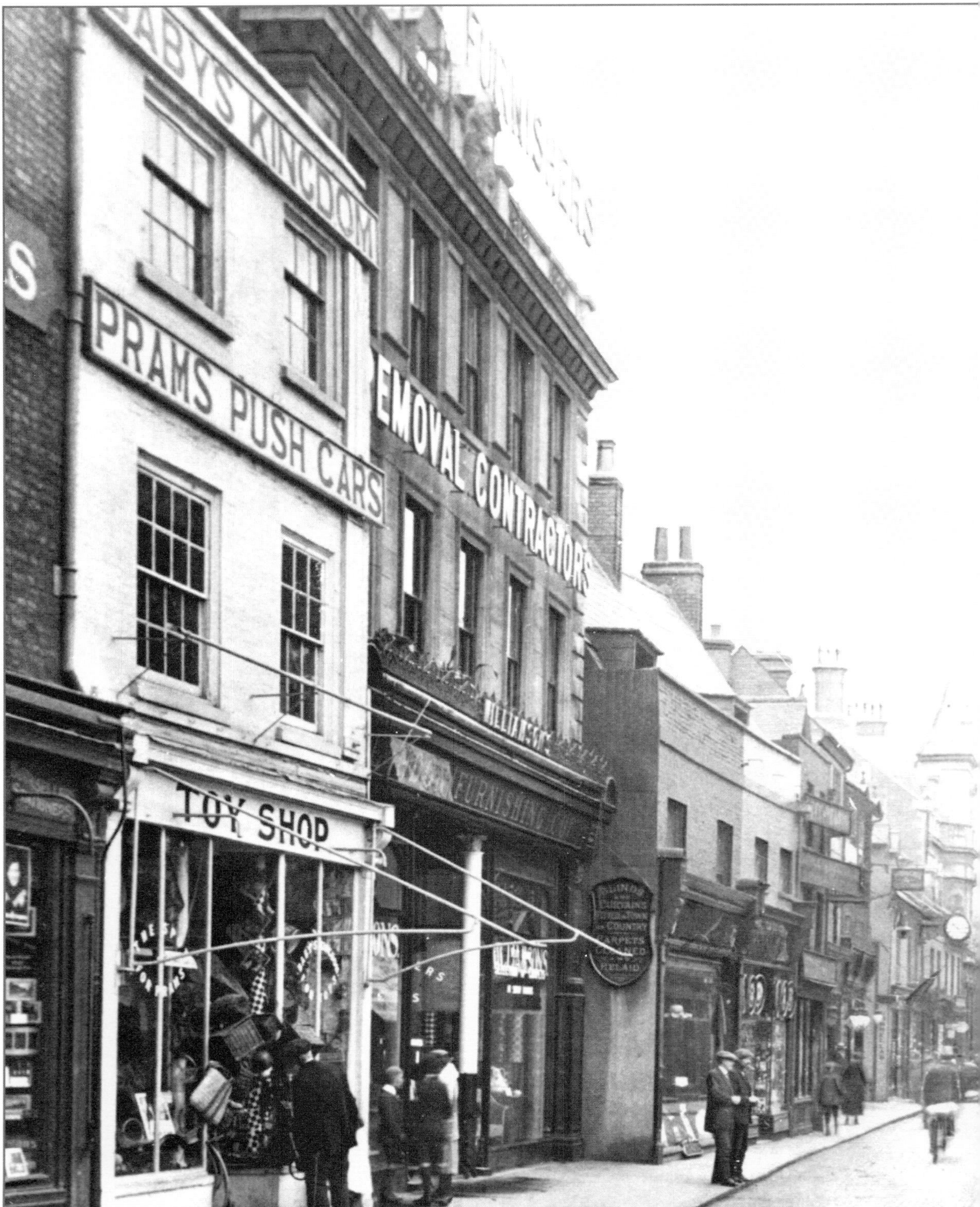
ABY'S KINGDOM
PRAMS PUSH CARS
EMOVAL CONTRACTORS
TOY SHOP

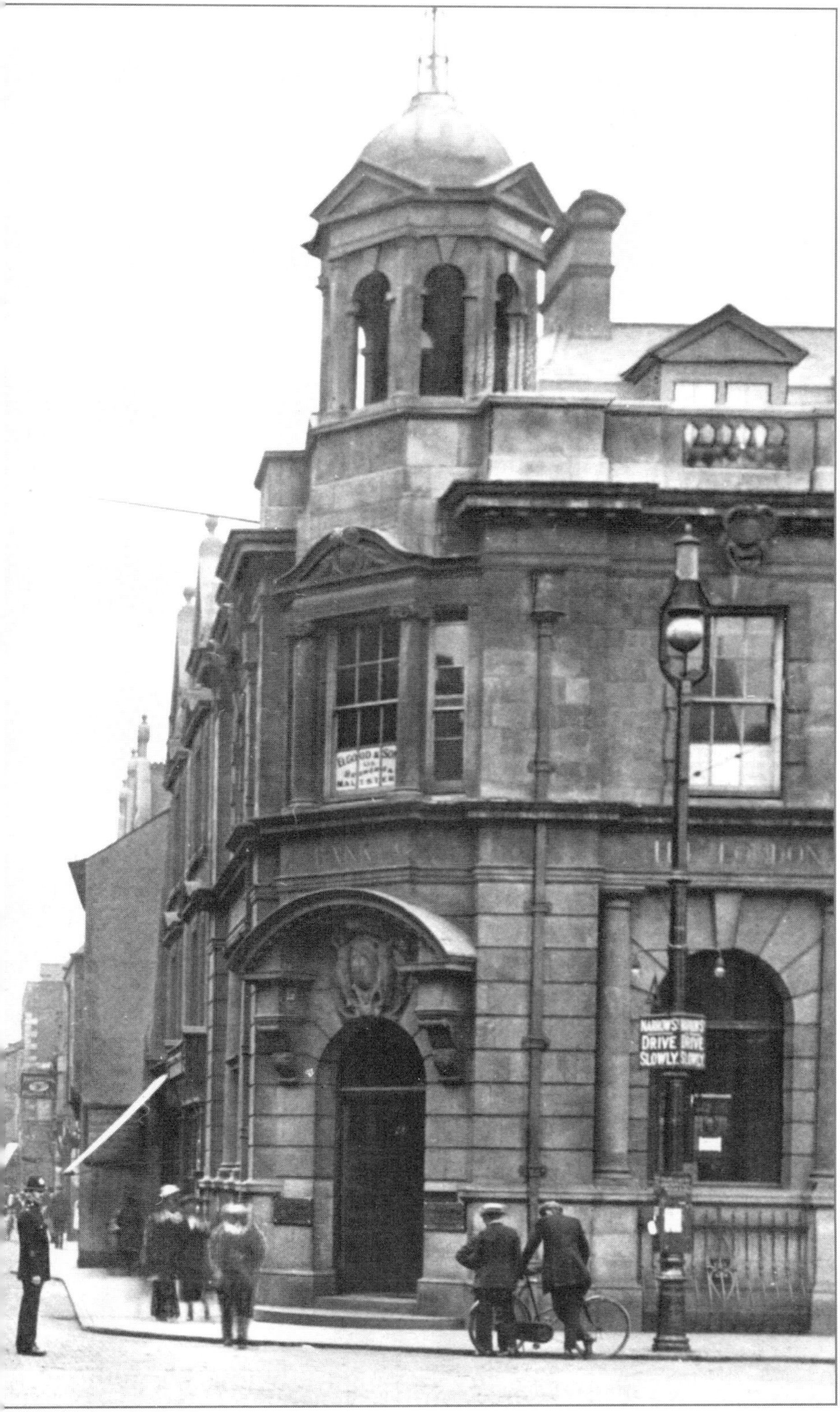

Narrow Street 1919

69094

Narrow Street was closed off at the turn of the century to control an election night mob. Alas, it is no more since widening and amalgamation with Bridge Street in the 1930s to improve access to the new council buildings. Imagine being able to walk into all those old shops now - what ancient wonders to behold! The bank is still there, and is now an HSBC.

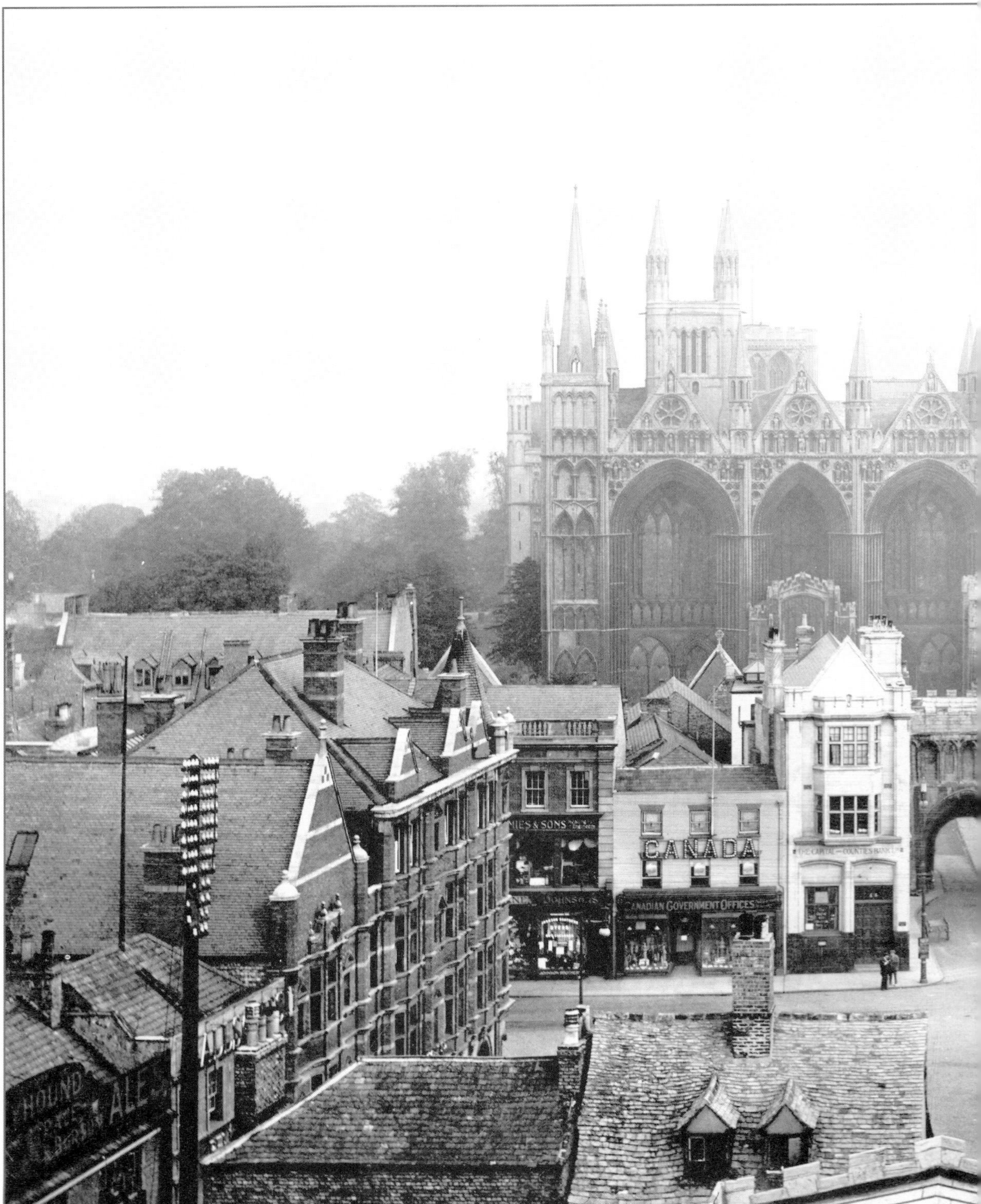
CANADA
CANADIAN GOVERNMENT OFFICES
ALE

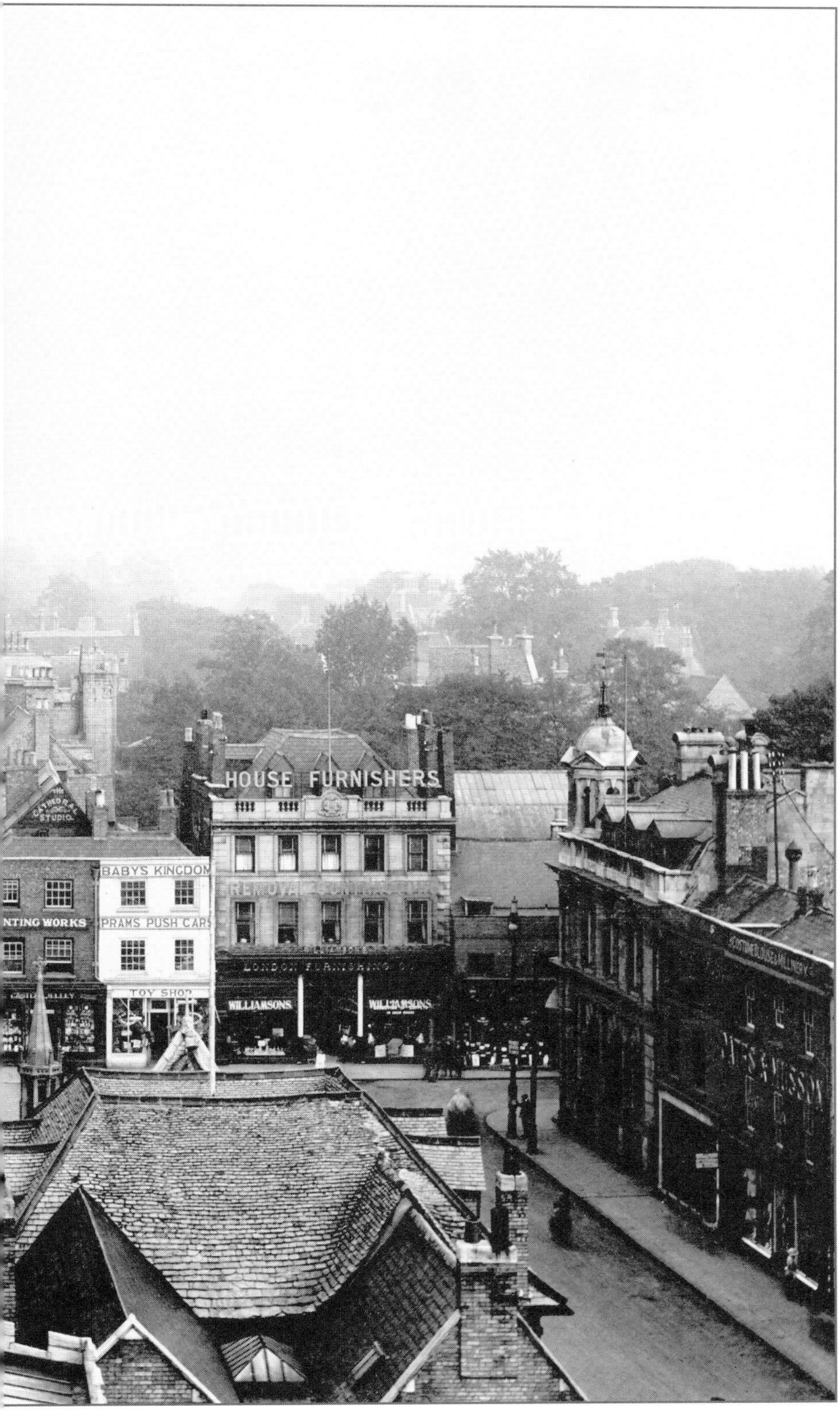

Cathedral Square 1919 69081
This view, taken from St John's Church across Cathedral Square, shows the Canadian Government offices next door to the Capital and Counties Bank, St Nicholas' Gate, the print works, a toy shop and the London Furnishing Co. The Cathedral's bulk rises among lush greenery in the background.

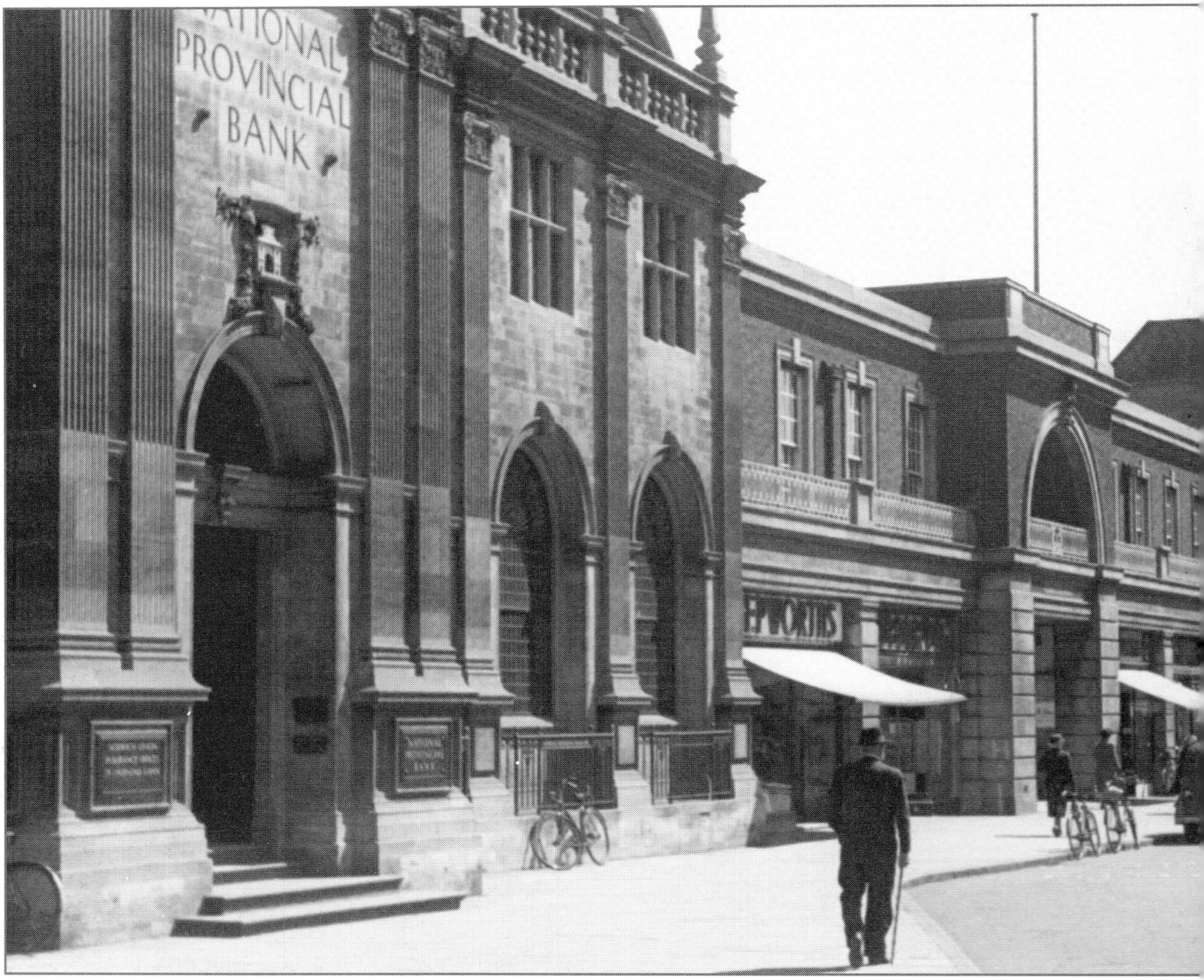

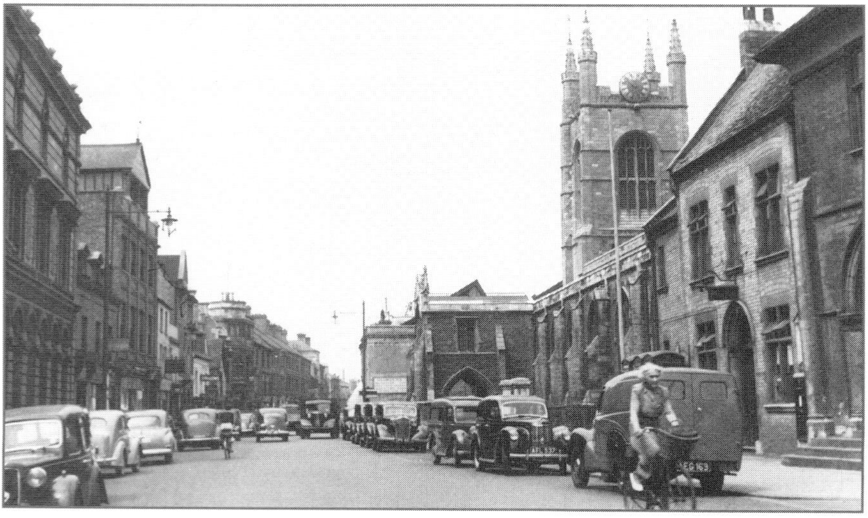

Church Street c1955

P47048

The ancient Guildhall and St John's Church loom large, evoking the city's ancient past. A future awaits, but the closest sign here of modern styling is in the faired-in headlights of the Ford Prefect parked just behind the passing cyclist - a stately soul, basket ready for the shopping.

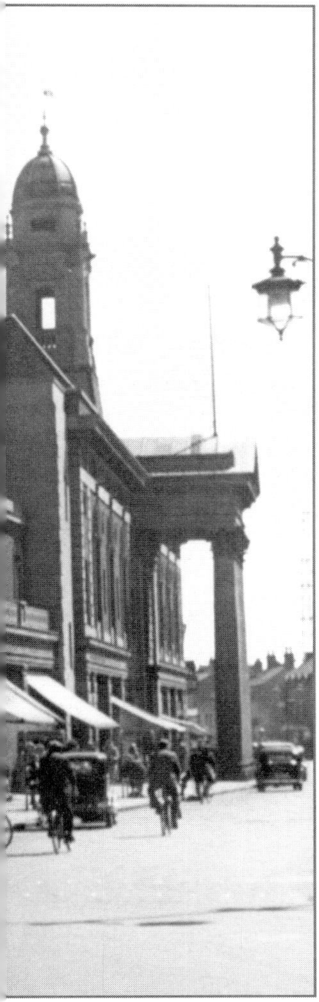

◄ **Bridge Street c1955**
P47015
Here we see some good solid architecture. A fine gent with a stick strolls toward Hepworths and a range of other sober shopfronts. Cars are few, and all rather dark. The stately council offices reflect 1930s ideas of grandeur, and the pylon reminds us that the river and the power station are not far down the road.

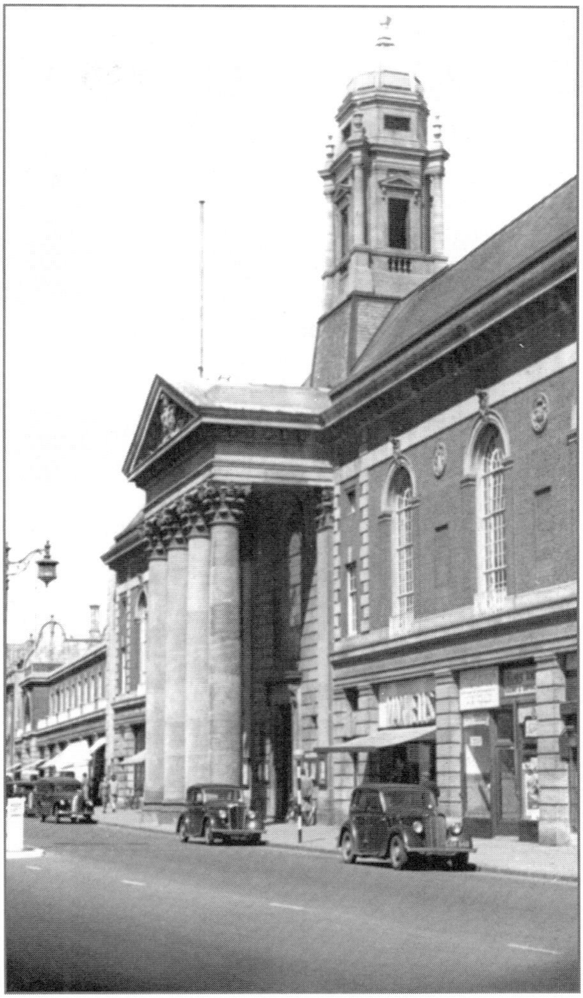

The Town Hall c1955 ►
P47017
We are looking up Bridge Street, and some rather splendid cars of the pre-war age can be seen. A sunny day prevails, and snow-white blinds are drawn down to protect the window displays.

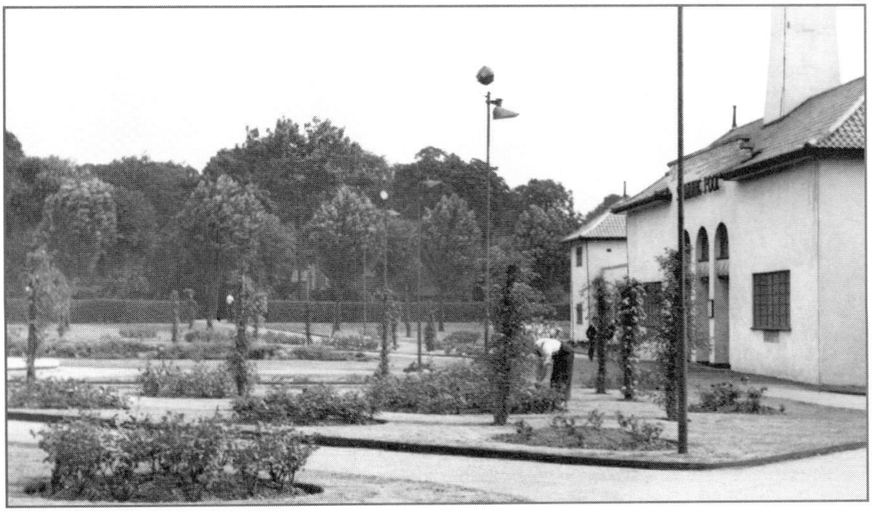

◄ **The Swimming Pool c1955** P47042
When this view was taken, it was nearly 20 years after the opening of the pool in Bishop's Road. Complete with diving board and under-water illumination, this facility was Hermione Longton's favourite haunt during school holidays. 'We used to have three pennies to buy a cup of Oxo in a white cup, which was very welcome when you were cold, and a penny bag of crisps. Another two pennies bought a bus ride back to New England'.

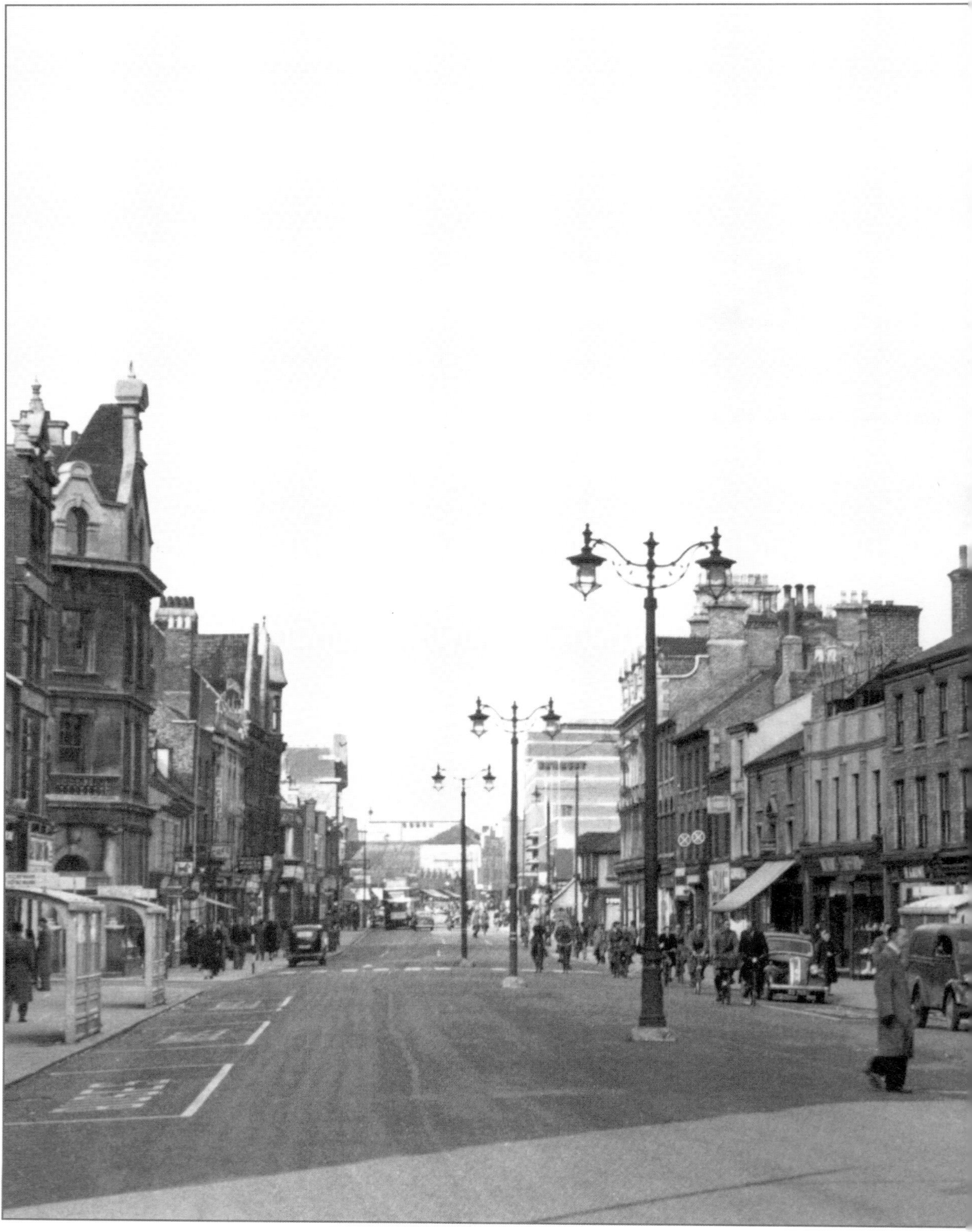

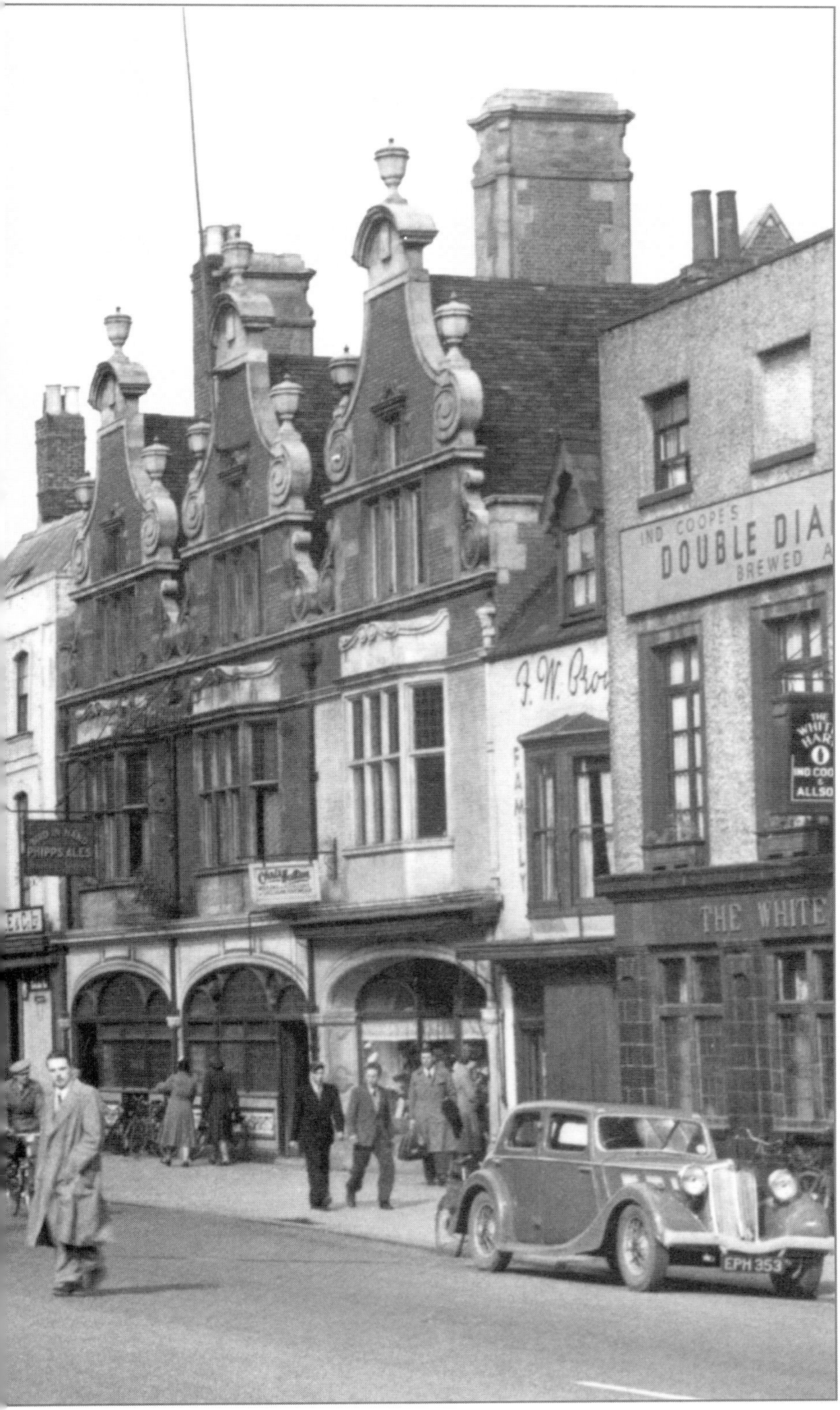

Long Causeway c1955
P47053
Here we have a clear view along to Broadway, where once there was a library and the Theatre Royal. Two elegant cars adorn the kerbside: a Triumph Dolomite, and Austin Atlantic Convertible - so named because it was aimed at the US market. Both were great names, now long gone, along with good old Double Diamond beer, then available in the pub, as we can see from the sign on the right; it was said to work wonders, according to the fast-growing advertising industry.

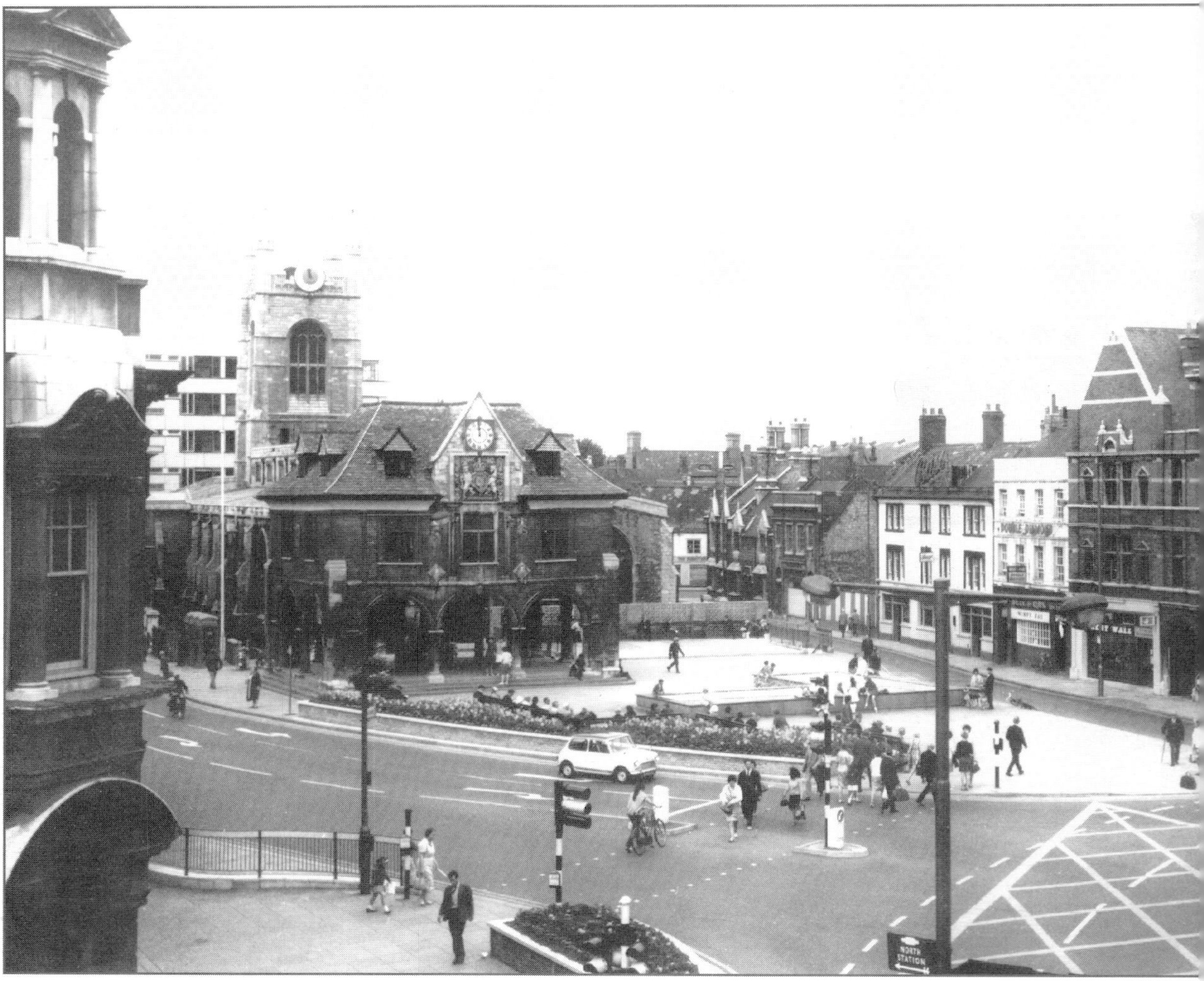

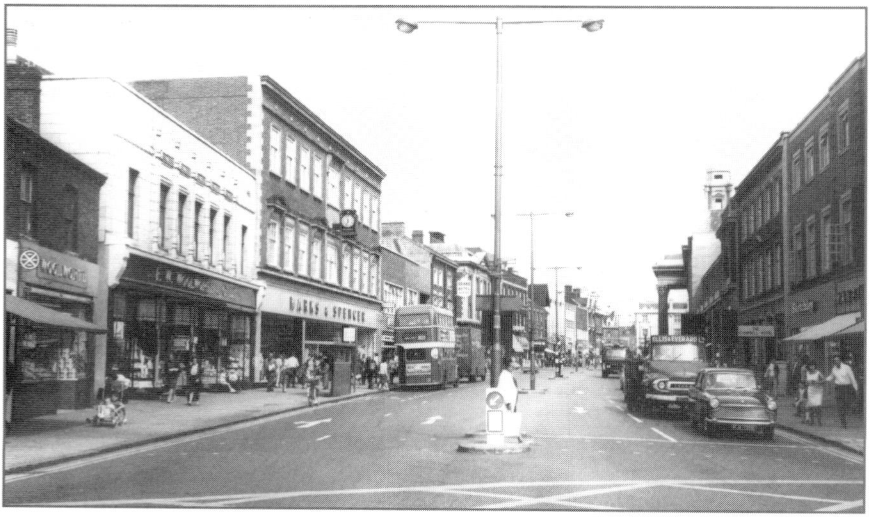

◄ **Bridge Street c1965**

P47068

Mac Fisheries, far left, was a regular on TV ads; Marks and Spencer's, built on the City Cinema site, has been open a year, next to Woolworth's, the other High Street favourite. Eastern Counties ran the bus services from 1913 when they took over the trams; here, they are supplying transport home for loaded shoppers without access to a car. More affluent visitors could board at the Grand Hotel opposite the Town Hall for £30 a week.

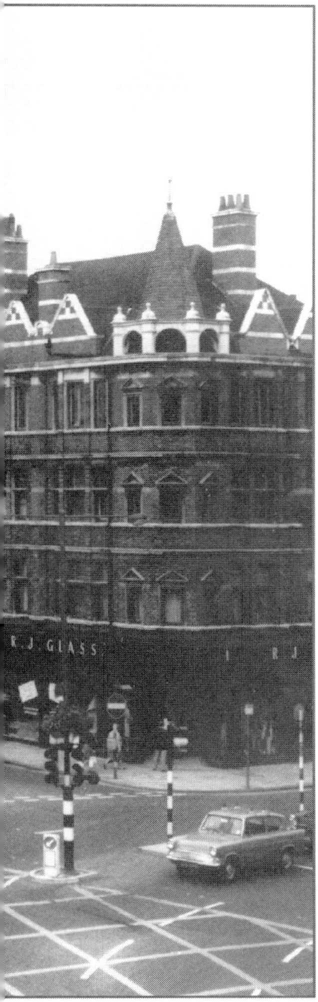

Cathedral Square and the Guildhall c1965
P47070
This is a good view of Bridge Street, showing a new-style box junction devised to cope with increasing traffic. R J Glass dominates the scene; the building survived 1970s redevelopment. The Wimpy Bar almost next door was very much 60s cool, and the new Mini exiting Church Street was for the most with it dudes!

Church Street c1965 P47080
Church Street has changed a bit in this view (compare it with picture No 47048). A large building has replaced the Corn Exchange, and overshadows the 15th-century church tower; it met the growing needs of the Norwich Union and the Post Office. W J Brown's seedsmiths are thriving, centre left. The former Burlington stores, just beyond Cross Street, has lost its turret and become a bar.

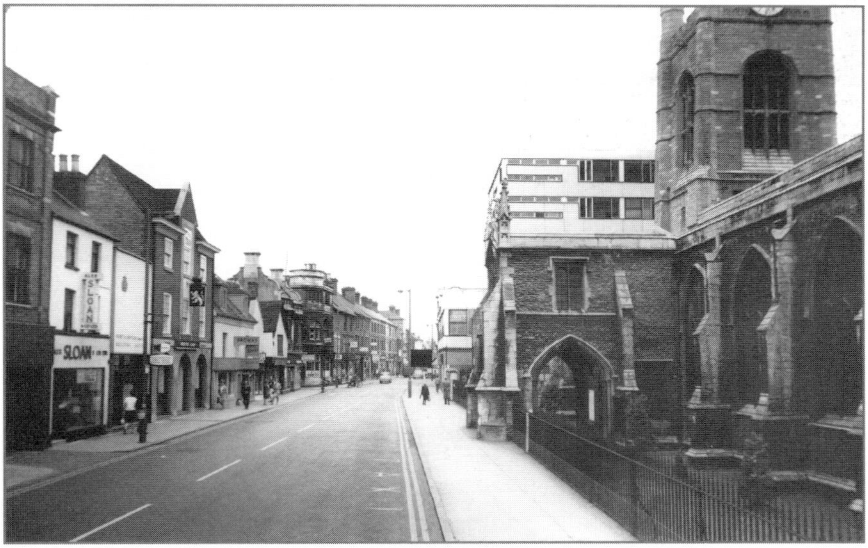

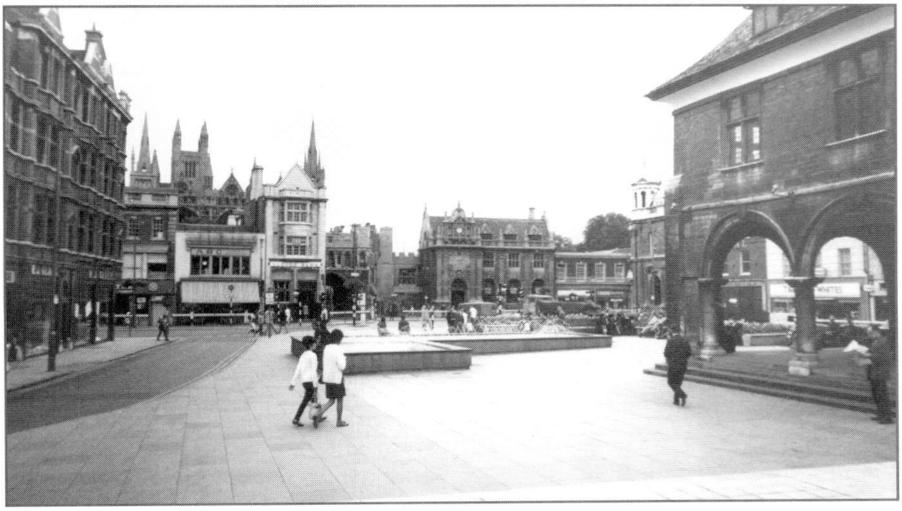

Cathedral Square and the Guildhall c1965
P47077
The Canada offices have given way to a fashion warehouse, and Lloyds have taken over the Capital and Counties Bank in this age of mergers; it also affected Timothy Whites, visible through the arches. White's became part of the Boots empire before fading from view.

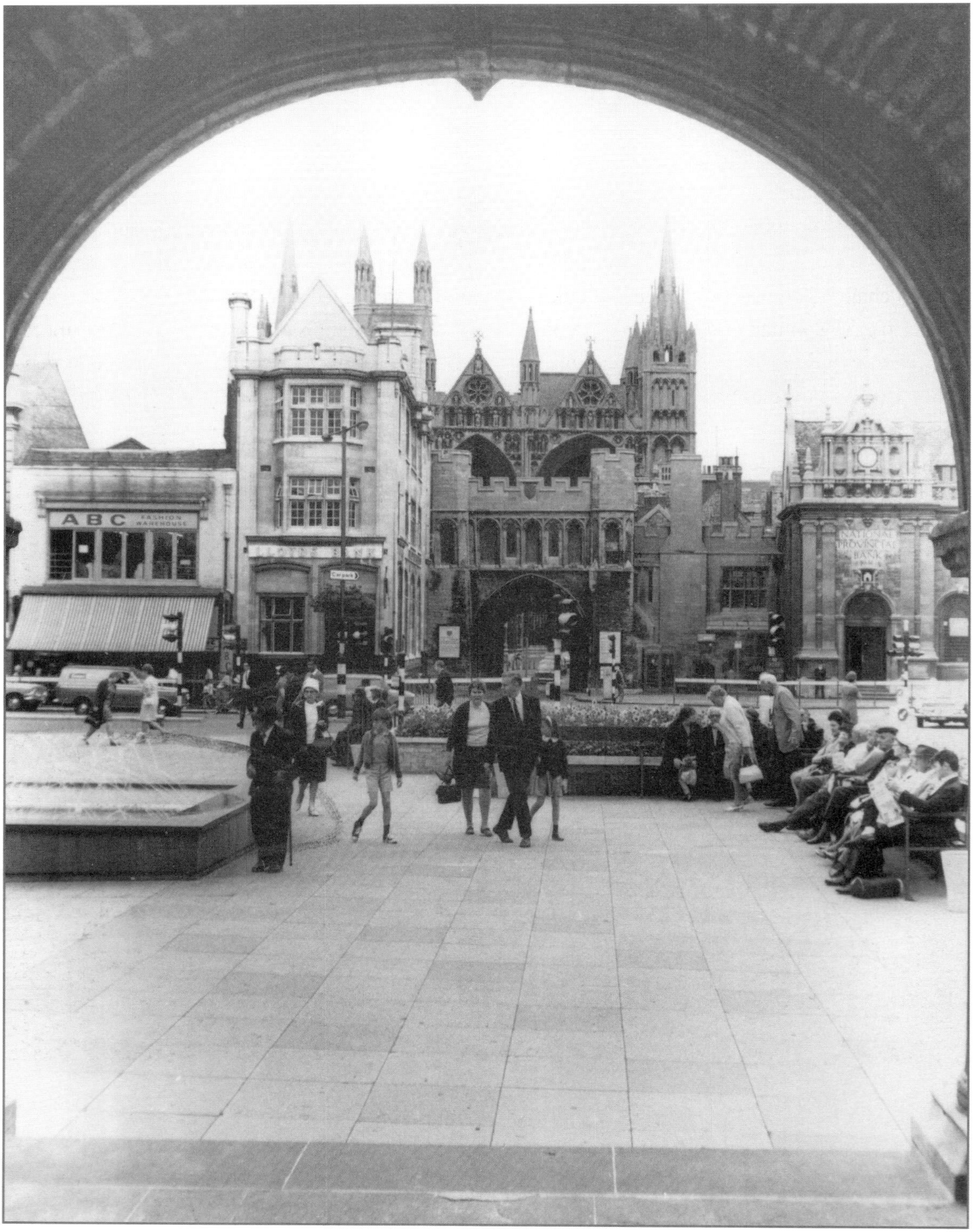

Cathedral Square c1965 P47076

This is an interesting view across a busy Square, framed by the Guildhall Arches; it is reminiscent of the view from the ancient butter market held here, when women sold butter, eggs, milk and poultry.

About Belief

Christianity began as the ideas and words of one man effectively challenged an established outlook to become the dominant ideology across Europe. Though challenged today by science and quick-fix politicians, religion had originally given purpose and order to human affairs. Symbols and places of worship were necessary to remind ordinary people of God's omnipresence and of their duty to his chosen representatives on earth - that is, those who had established power.

And so we gained Peterborough Cathedral, Thorney Abbey, Crowland Abbey and many more churches across the fens. St Wendreda at March is a fine example, famous for its double ►

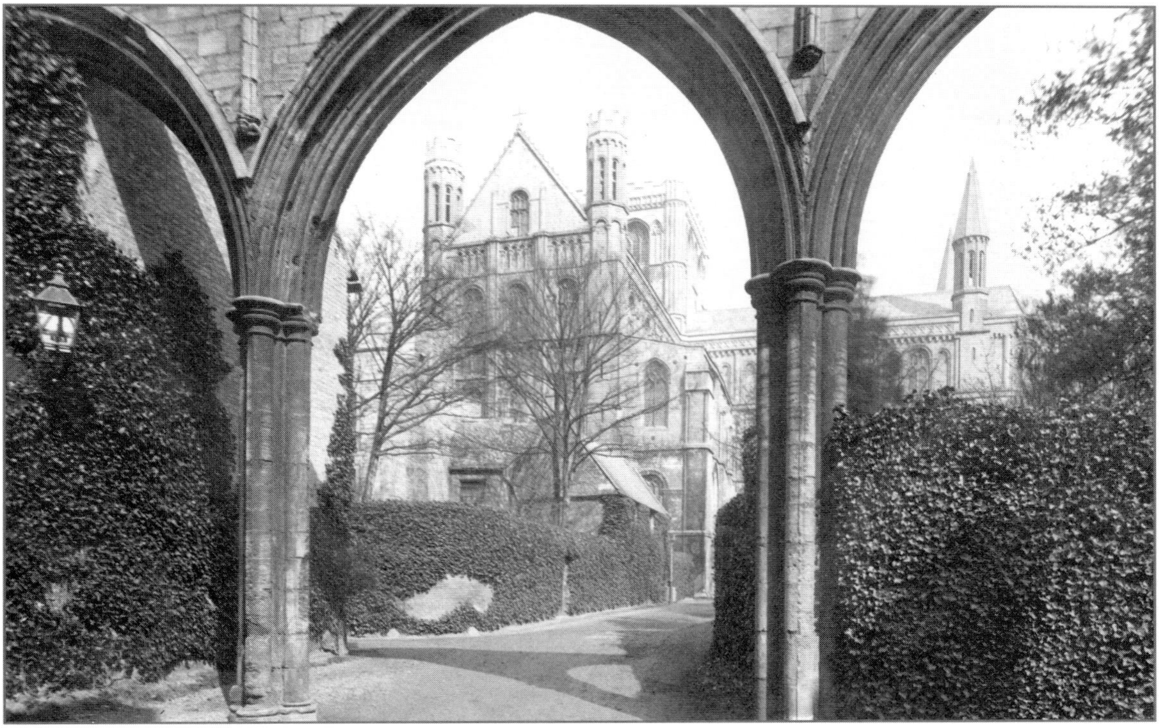

The Infirmary Arches 1890 24444

Following a public meeting, and the forming of a subscription list in 1815, the process of establishing a public dispensary began. Subscribers could recommend one patient per guinea subscribed. Many patients travelled from the countryside, necessitating accommodation which was found in Milton Street to serve as an infirmary. Bigger premises were found in Priestgate in 1856.

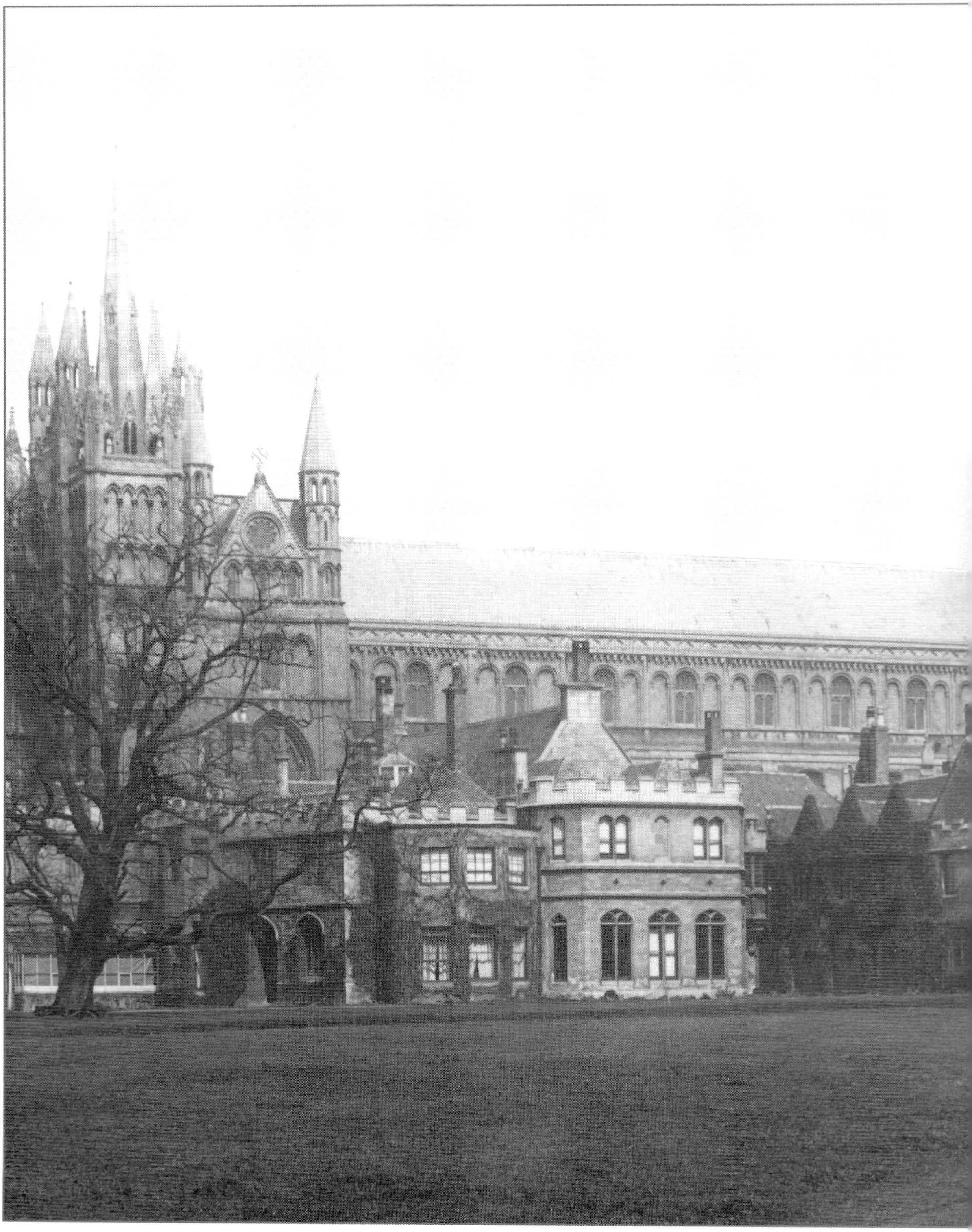

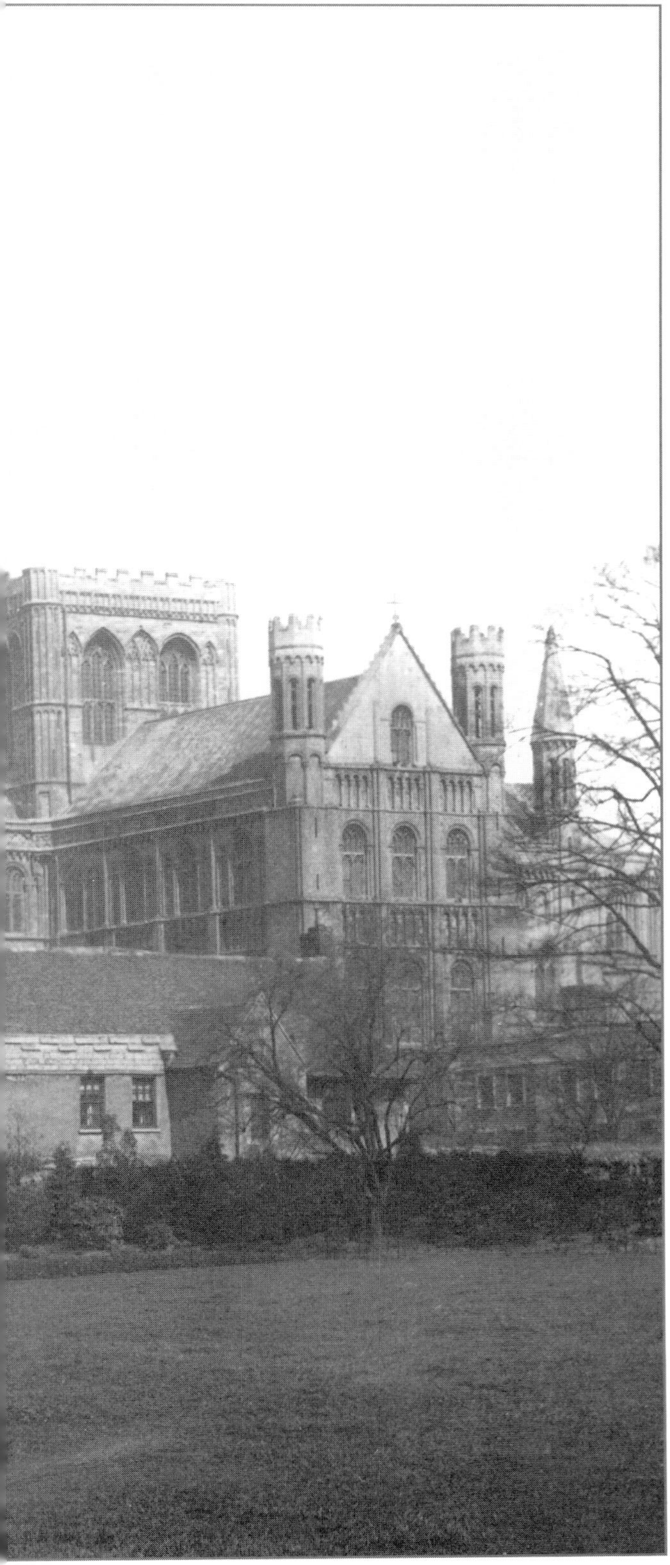

hammerbeam roof with many carved angels. Pagan Viking invaders fought the faith, but offered no better idea than a little trade. Stability waited for the Vikings' Norman descendants. Catholicism was despatched by Henry VIII; James II's attempts to revive it and make it uniform only encouraged dissent and rebellion. People wanted faith and purpose, but also some individuality. Freedom, however, is often recognition of necessity, and must give way to compromise.

During the 19th century local farming faced decline, while railways and engineering boomed around the city. Traditional woolcombing was doomed. Machine wreckers fought against mechanisation on the land. The old feudal order, so ruthlessly established and only weakly opposed locally by the likes of Hereward the Wake (said to be buried at Crowland Abbey), had had a long reign; but now it was under threat. The Fitzwilliam family rode the tide of change. They had owned property in the city since the Great Rebellion, which was handy for influencing votes. Democracy struggled against the forces of conservatism and exploitation, while Britain was being swept along by the energy of its innovators and the needs of a growing empire. New industries generated new beliefs, such ▶

The Cathedral and the Bishop's Palace 1890
24435
Here we see an island of upper-class tranquillity in an increasingly industrial town. The low-lying building is still a haven, with its many little pinnacles, spires and squat square tower.

as the local Co-op movement. Paternalistic employers like Perkins, Brotherhood Engineering and the Stewarts, who eventually controlled the London Brick Company, set new standards for the future. Two world wars challenged the notion of God's goodwill, brought out the insularity of local folk and ultimately crumbled the old-established ways. The number of ancient Northamptonshire families had already declined from 350 to 20 by 1906. After 1945, the changes accelerated, and the city had to look outward for its future and expansion; this trend was reflected across the district. London Brick have been symbolic of the new order of belief in international capitalism. When Hansons made their takeover bid in December 1983, they had a turnover of £1,848 million across the world and offered shareholders a price they could not refuse. Their effect on London Brick has not been without local impact. International capital calls the tune and pays the piper. In this environment, there is always the danger that local areas will lose their character.

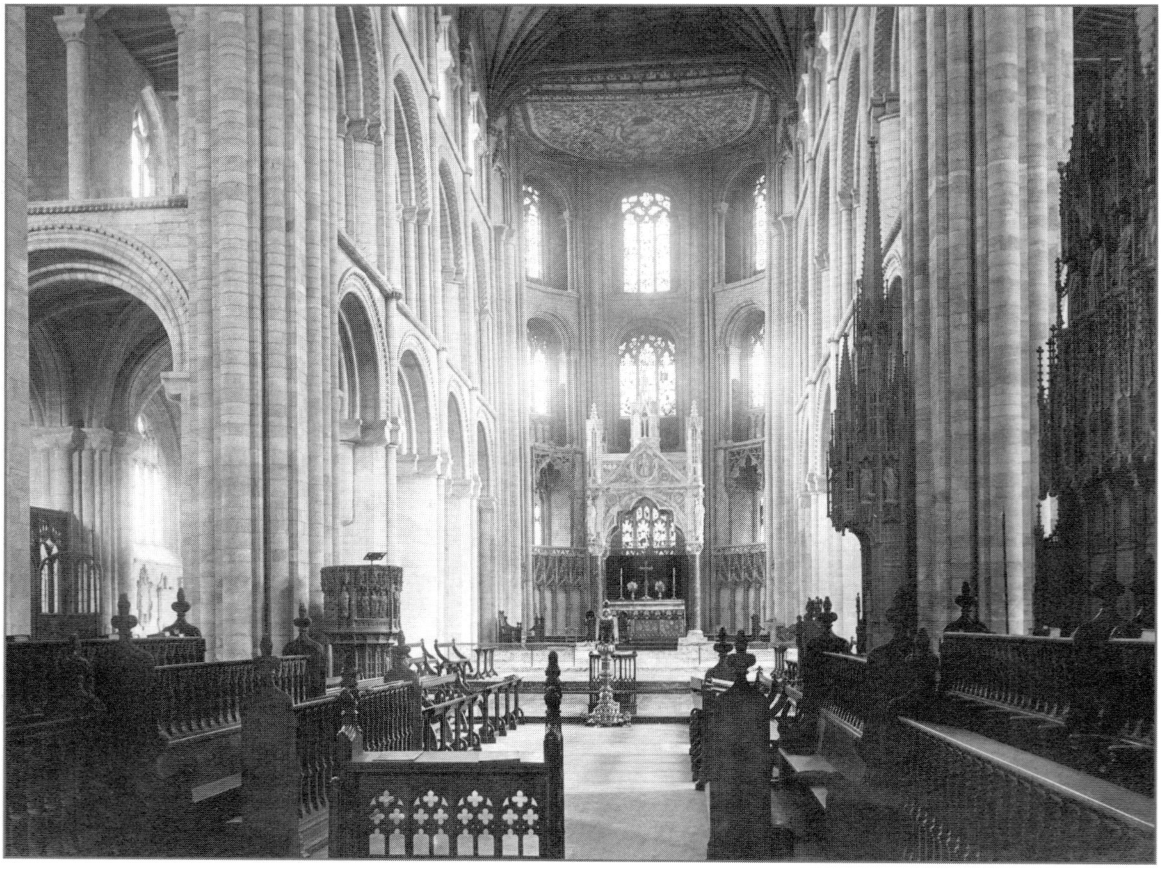

The Cathedral, Choir East 1894 34821

Hermione Longton recalls: 'I still feel emotional, going out into the Cathedral, thinking of my father as a little boy. He was so privileged, as a working-class boy, to be selected for a scholarship at King's Choir School and singing in the choir. But he gave up his music studies to work for the London Brick Company'.

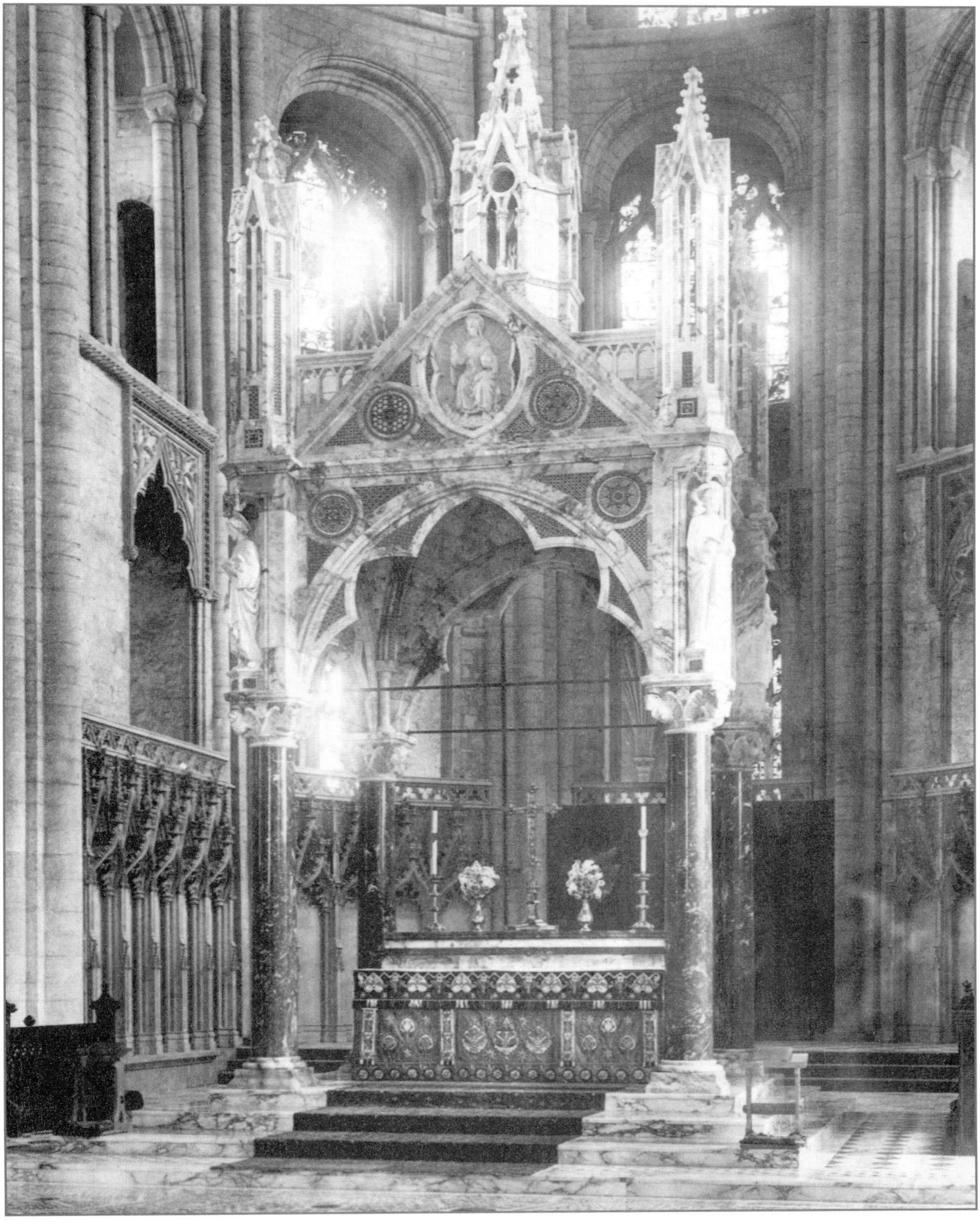

The Cathedral, The Reredos 1894 34827
The Cathedral is renowned for its abundant light and its simplicity of style. John Loughborough Pearson, a leading church architect, worked on the building during this period, and was responsible for this sumptuous baldachino (the canopy over the altar).

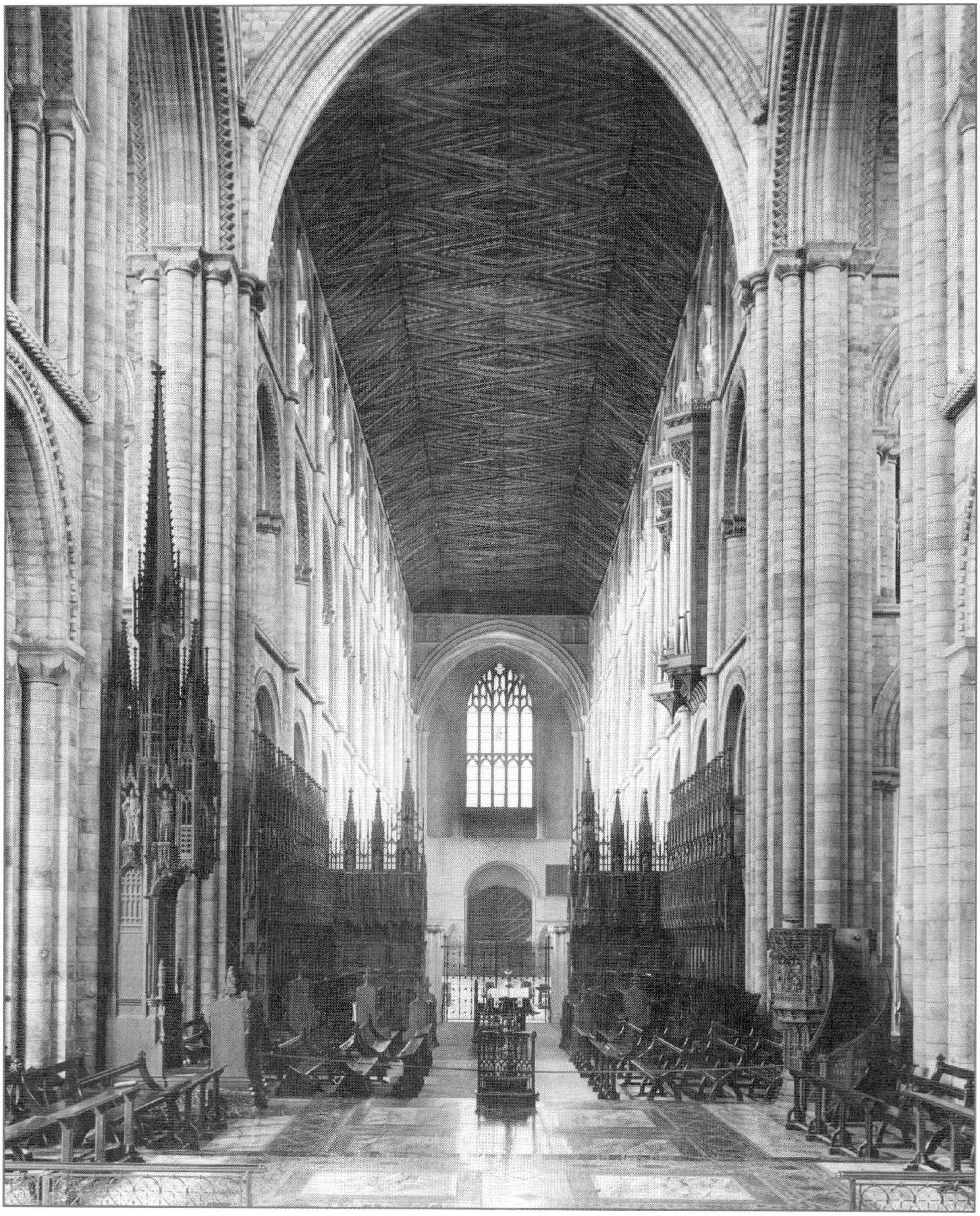

The Cathedral, Choir West 1894 34824
Mary Queen of Scots, beheaded a few miles away at Fotheringay in 1587, was buried in the south choir aisle - she was later removed to Westminster by her son James I. A portrait of her gravedigger, Robert Scarlett, who lived to be 98, was placed at the west end of the nave.

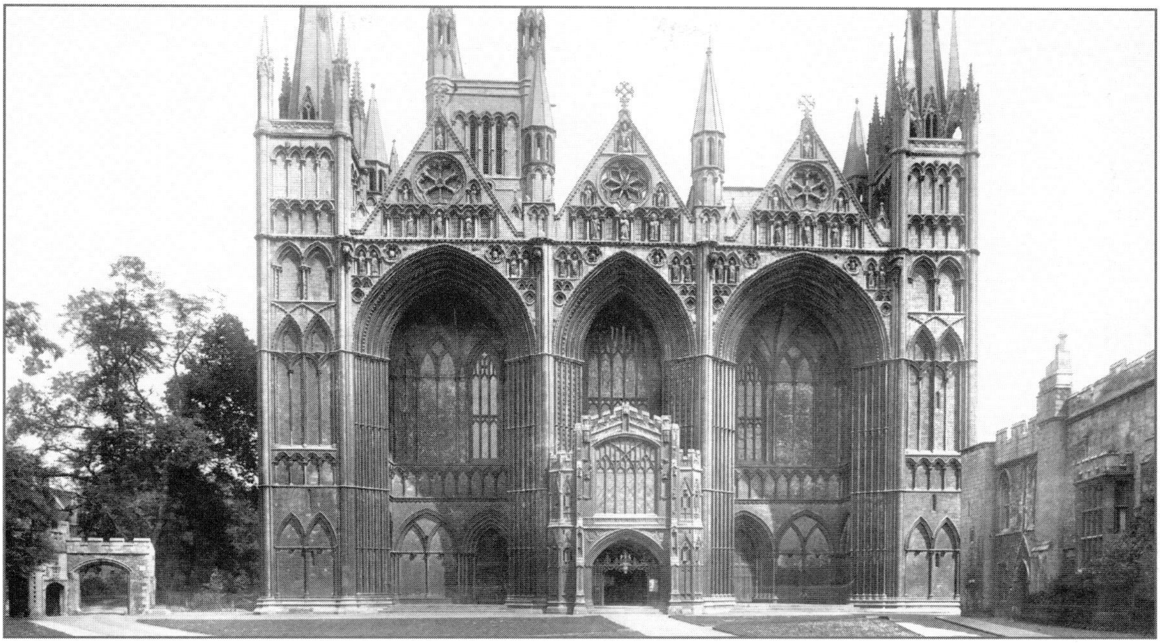

The Cathedral, West Front 1904 51551
This is certainly one of the three greatest west fronts in England. Notice the slim towers with tapering spires on either side. Pinnacles add to the iced cake effect. The three great arches, topped by tiny wheel windows and decorated with profuse carvings, are overwhelming.

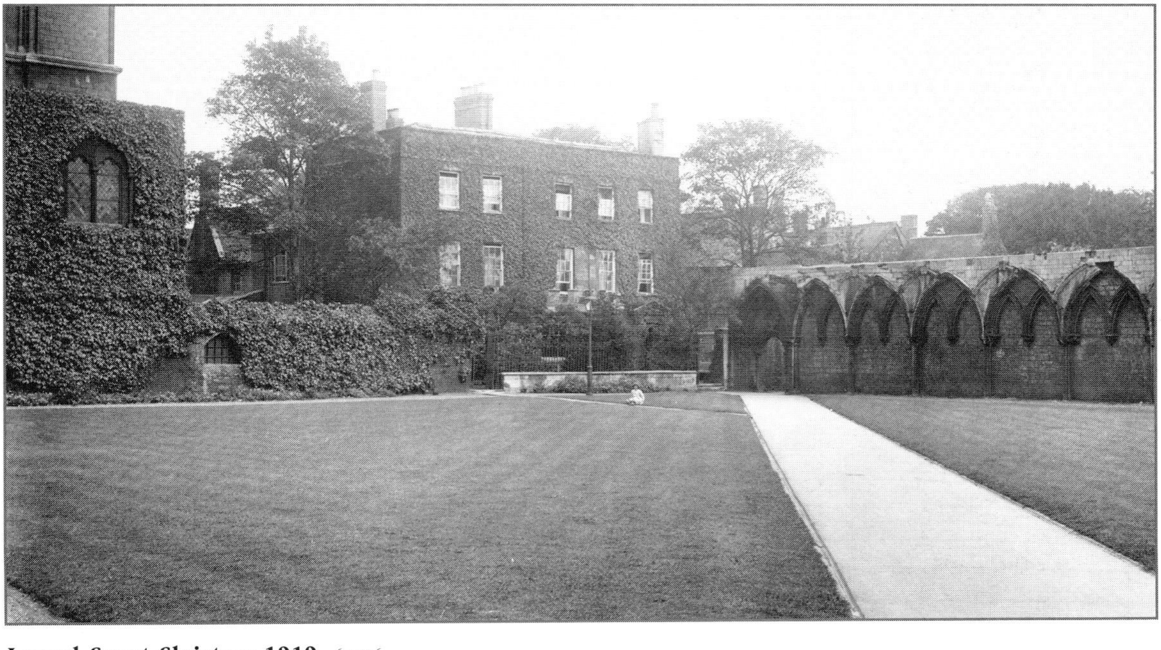

Laurel Court Cloisters 1919 69086
This must have been a rarefied atmosphere for clerics and scholars in a world only just recovering from the trauma of Britain's war with Germany. Incidentally, the cross from the prison grave of the former Laurel Court teacher, Edith Cavell, was recently presented to the Royal London Hospital Archives, along with the Union flag which draped her coffin and her last letter written to her fellow nurses.

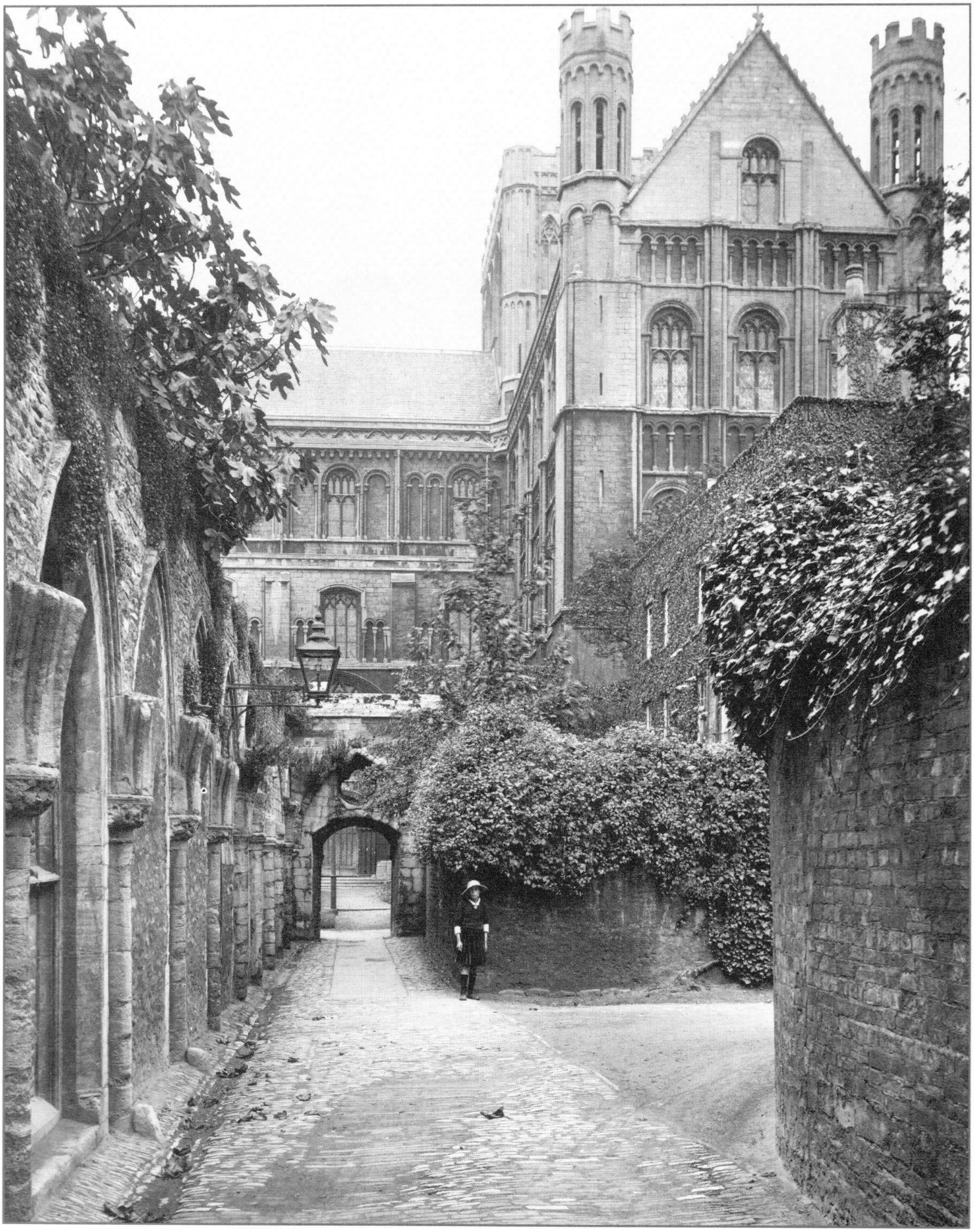

The Cathedral, The Slip 1919 69085
The slip, or slype, is a narrow passage leading past Laurel Court and the cloisters; it is a fairly confined area from which to admire the awesome church tower.

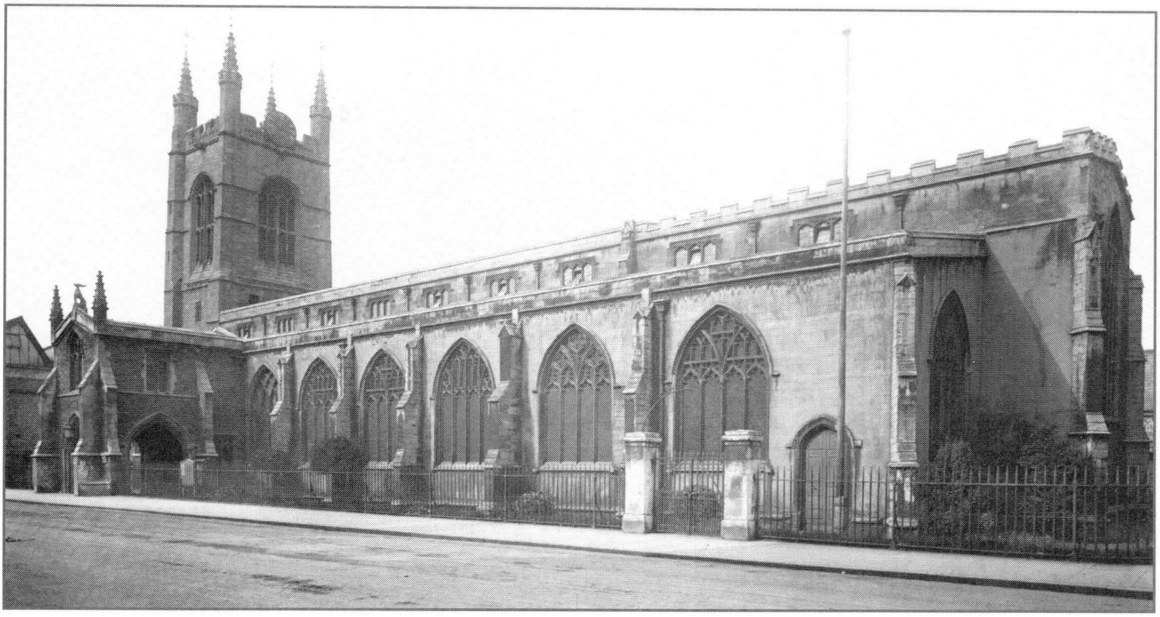

St John's Church 1919 69087

This is an unusually unobstructed view of St John's, before development boxed it in. This church replaced an older one following the Bishop of Lincoln's decision in 1402; the first mass was celebrated in 1407. The building included oak from the Abbot's park and stone from the nave of the recently-demolished Becket chapel; it had a tall lead-covered spire, which was demolished for safety reasons in the 19th century.

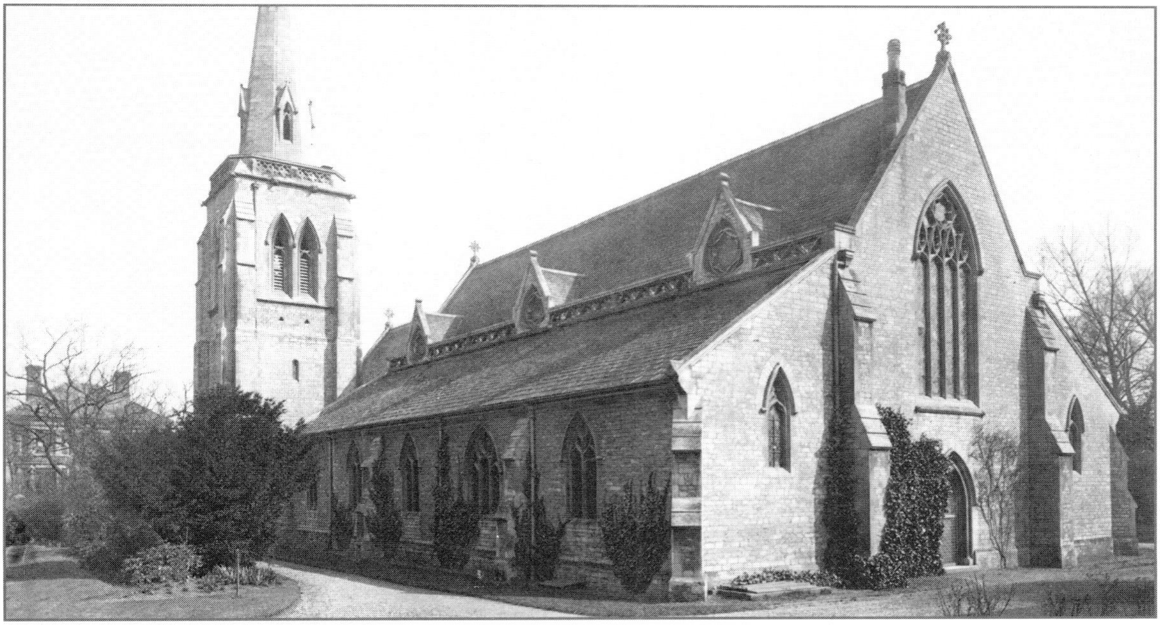

St Mark's Church 1890 24447

Railways had boosted industry and the city's growth from the middle of the 19th century; the expansion engulfed detached hamlets, thus creating more parishes, which were a basis for local government. Longthorpe became a separate parish in 1850. A parish to include New England was created in 1857, and St Mark's Church was built on the edge of Spital housing estate in Lincoln Road.

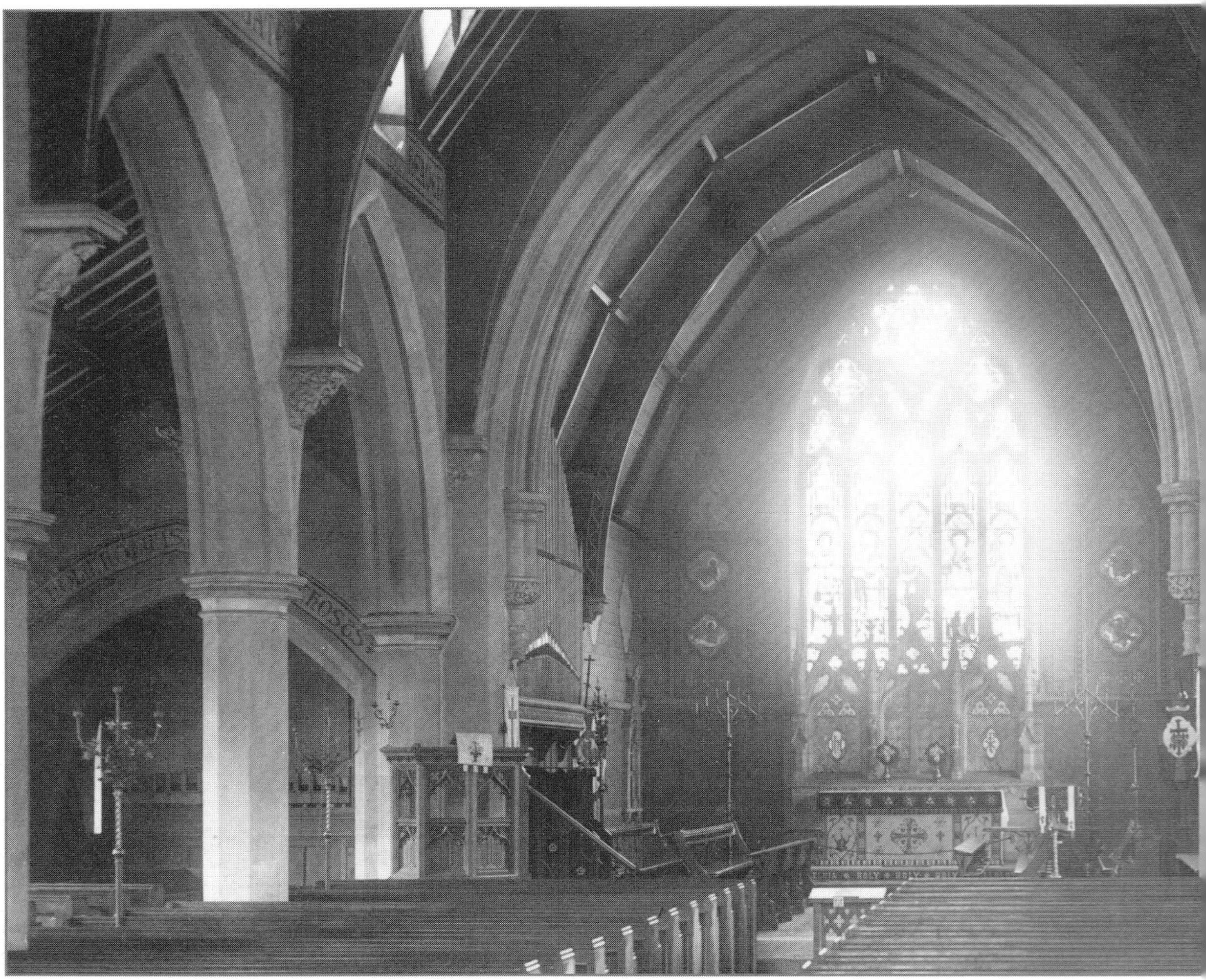

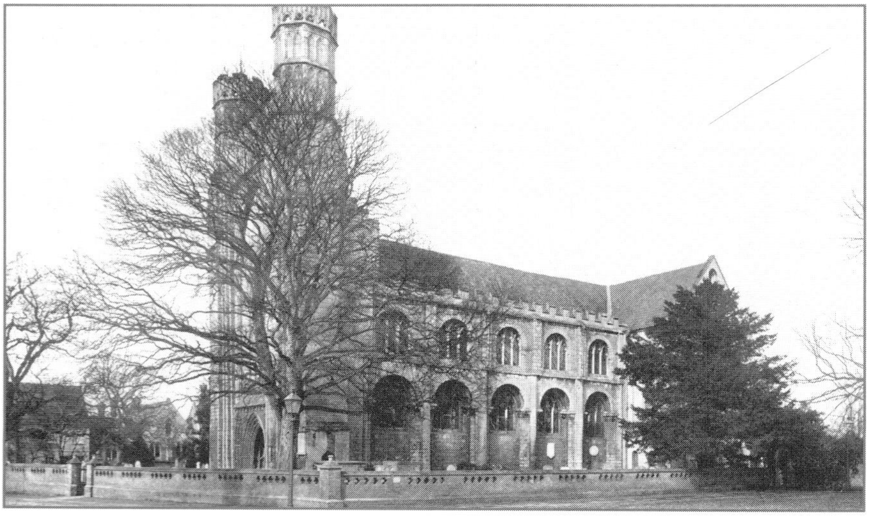

◄ **Thorney Abbey 1890**

24454

Guthlac, a Mercian royal warrior, came here on St Bartholomew's Day 699, having entered the monastery at Repton. He said that he would found his hermitage wherever his boat landed among the swamps. He anchored three-quarters of a mile from the present abbey. After Danish sacrilege in 972, the abbey was re-founded for Benedictine monks.

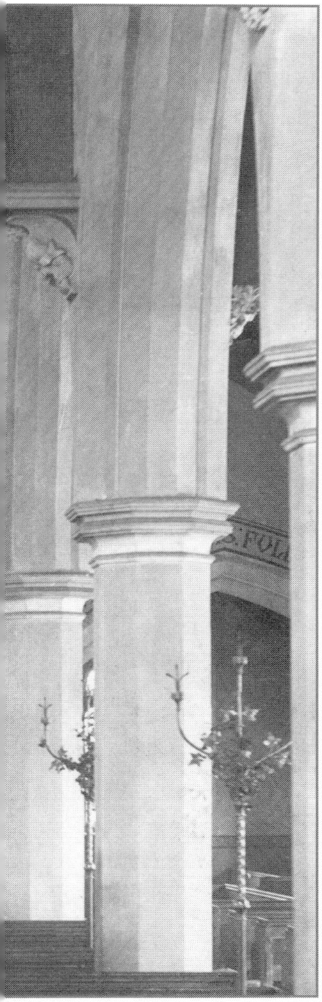

Interior of St Mark's Church 1890 24448
Norman church architecture set a trend for maximising light, and this church follows that stately tradition, very much in keeping with Peterborough's sense of style.

Castor The Church 1890 24457
This photograph shows the richly-carved Norman tower, among the finest in England. An inscription records the dedication of the church in 1124. The view today is little changed, even with sheep grazing in the churchyard.

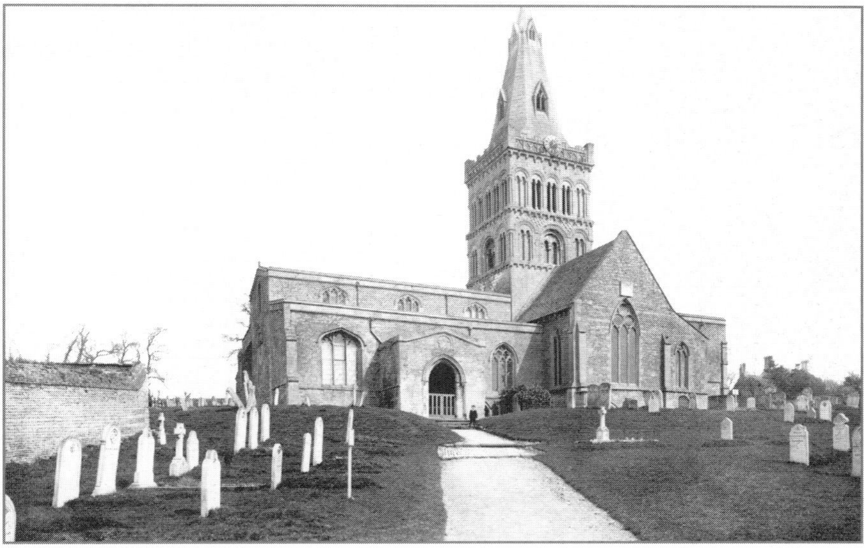

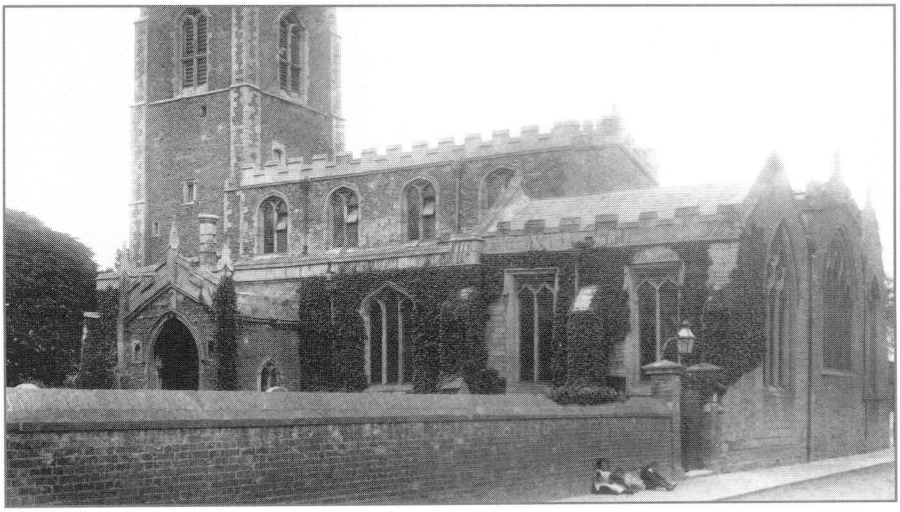

Whittlesey St Andrew's Church 1904 51564
This church is situated out in the fens. It is not a dramatic structure, but the Perpendicular and Georgian features create pleasant effects. The urchins on the pavement apparently have little to do, so perhaps this is Sunday.

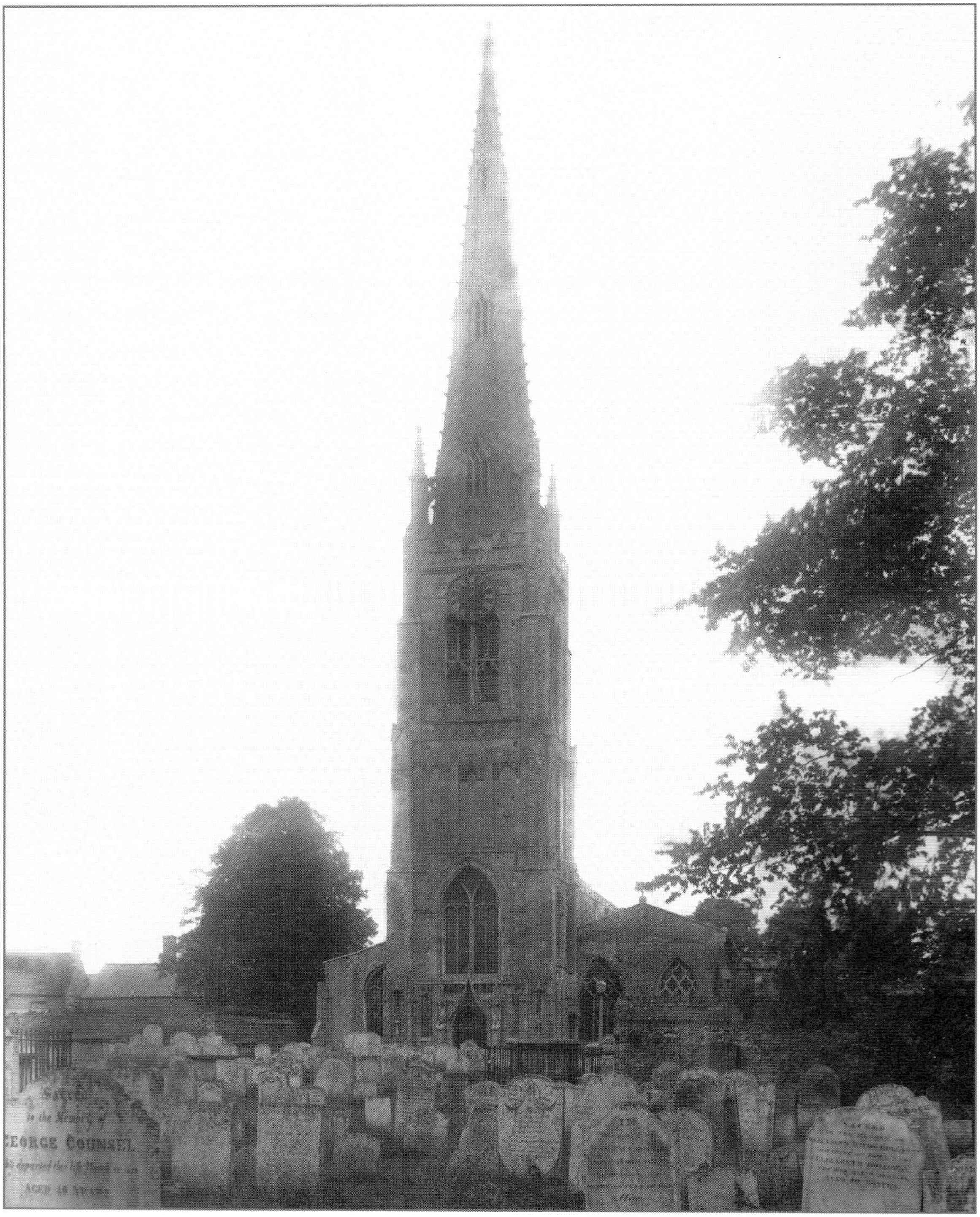

Whittlesey, The Church 1904 51563
St Mary's has a fine 15th-century tower and a crocketed spire. The packed graveyard reminds us that all things are temporary. Nowadays, old stones have been removed to the periphery, and some have been targeted by vandals with spray cans.

Waterways

The River Nene, rising to the south near Northampton, dominates the region; it is crucial to the draining of the fens, and encourages the population into the fertile area south of Peterborough. At Castor the remains of a Roman wharf were revealed. The population was more sparse closer to the city and in the fens. Drainage north of the city was much improved and altered following the early works of Vermuyden.

A curious outcome of these steady improvements is evident at Crowland, where a bridge stands on dry land. Apparently without purpose, it makes sense only if we recall that Crowland was once a group of islands where the main streets were waterways. The River Welland divided into two streams. One passed the Abbey on the south side and was used for sanitation and sewage; it was called Catt-Water drain, and discharged into the Nene. The main branch continued toward Spalding. The bridge was used to cross both streams - which still exist, arched over and serving as local sewers.

The Nene at March makes a pretty picture; in the past it has seen boat-building and much trade, ►

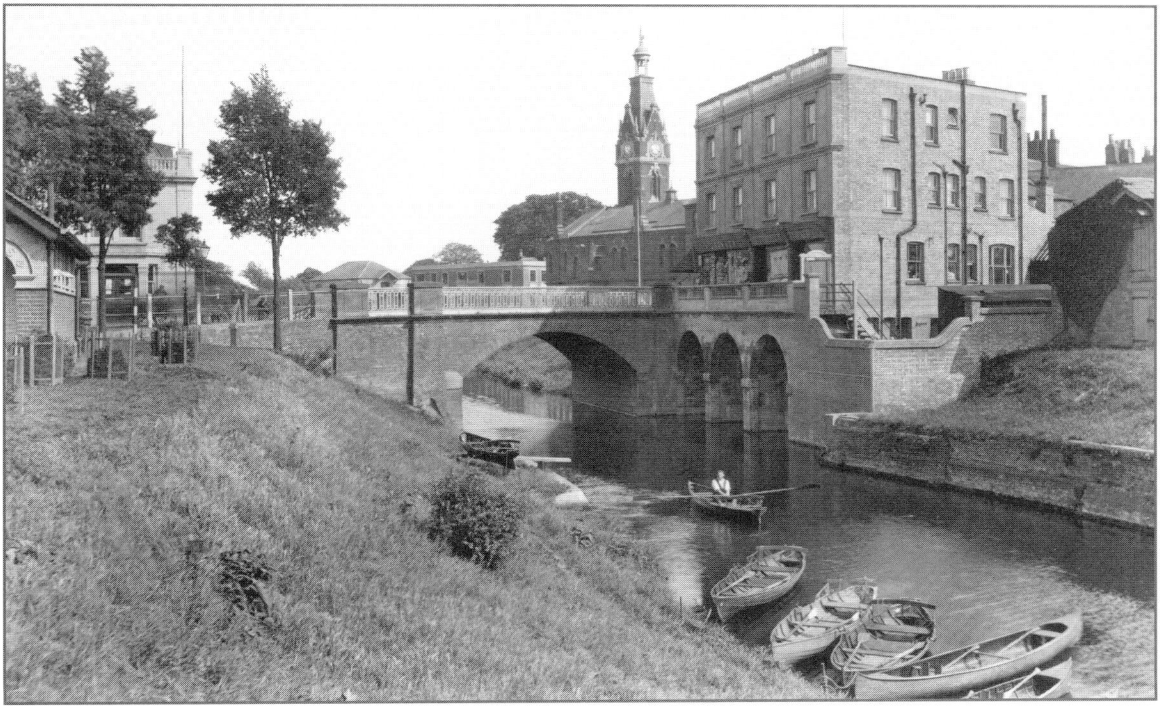

March, The Bridge from Nene Quay 1929 81913

This view, once open, is rather obscured today. The clock tower is typical of 19th-century municipal architecture, and befitted this market town in the Isle of Ely.

but it is now a place for pleasure craft. Peterborough itself had pride of place as the river's main port; in early days, the river was also the city's sewer. Drainage was still medieval in the 19th century, and typhoid epidemics were a problem. At Woodston and Fletton sewage flowed directly into the river, but many city drains never reached that far, owing to inadequate fall. From Medeshamstede's beginnings the abbot controlled the river. An Act of Parliament in 1713 set out to make it navigable from Northampton to Peterborough, and eventually to connect with the canal network, thus boosting trade in coal, corn and malt. The scheme to reach Oundle was mooted in 1692, but the navigable river scheme did not reach Peterborough until 1760. The city grew busier, and so much traffic needed to cross the river that a wooden bridge on stone piers replaced the ford in 1308. Built by Abbot Godfrey of Crowland, this bridge survived until a new iron bridge was built by public subscription in 1860. During the Napoleonic wars, prisoners of war disembarked here to be marched to prison at Norman Cross. Meanwhile, barge traffic carried stone, until the railways usurped it. The present town bridge, twice as wide, opened in 1934. Though the river was well past its heyday in 1934, road traffic was burgeoning when the new bridge was opened. This was a fitting memorial for a river now ready for more gentle leisure craft; it pleases the eyes of those with moments to admire the waterside and the swans.

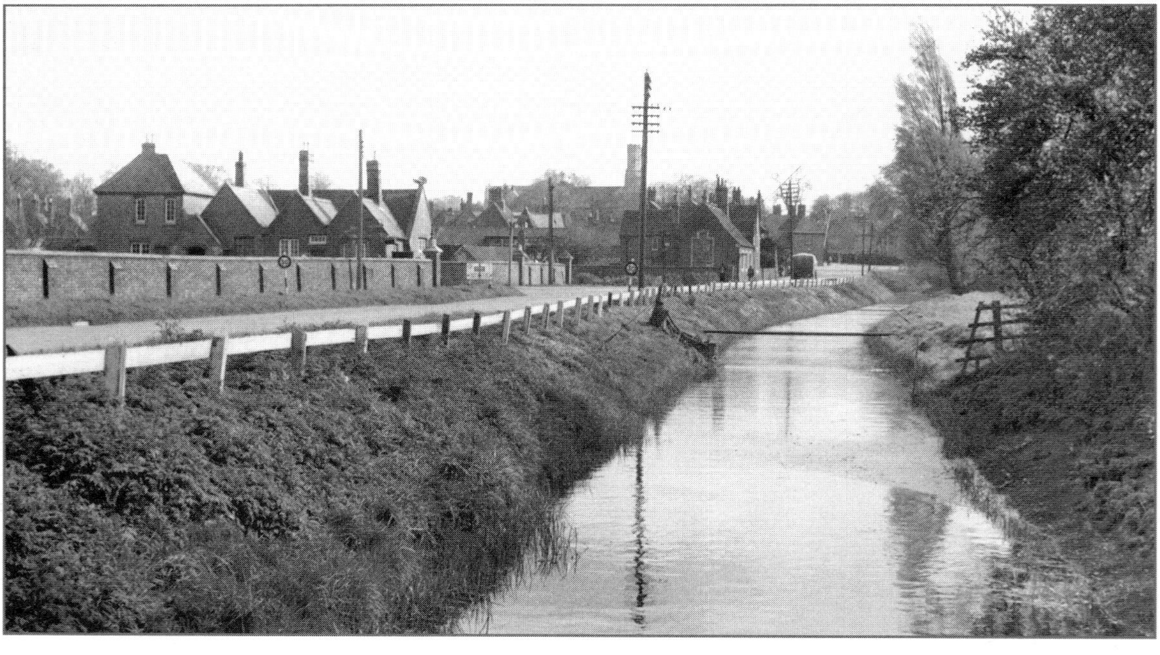

Thorney, The River c1955 T33012
This stream, an example of the artificially-straightened drainage pattern of the fens, drains land north-east of Peterborough, running into the Nene near the Wash. The view here looks toward the rear of The Rose and Crown pub on the A4, with the abbey church visible in the distance.

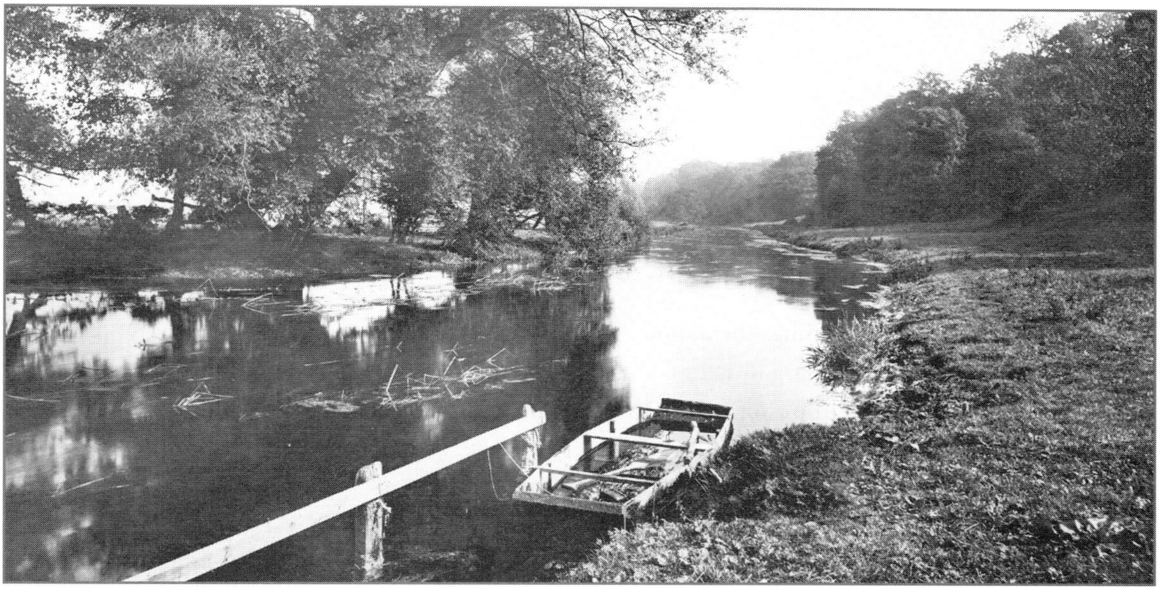

Alwalton Lynch 1919 69105

Ruby Hill, nee James, went courting here during the 1920s when this was still a village, rather than a suburb complete with a business park. Ruby recalls: 'I was in a pub with my boyfriend, a lady asked if he could play 'Liebestraum'. He did, he could play anything. We travelled by motorcycle. I was only 16, he was playing piano at a party and asked me out. I said you don't want to go out with a schoolgirl. We went to Milton Ferry, you could walk down to the fields'.

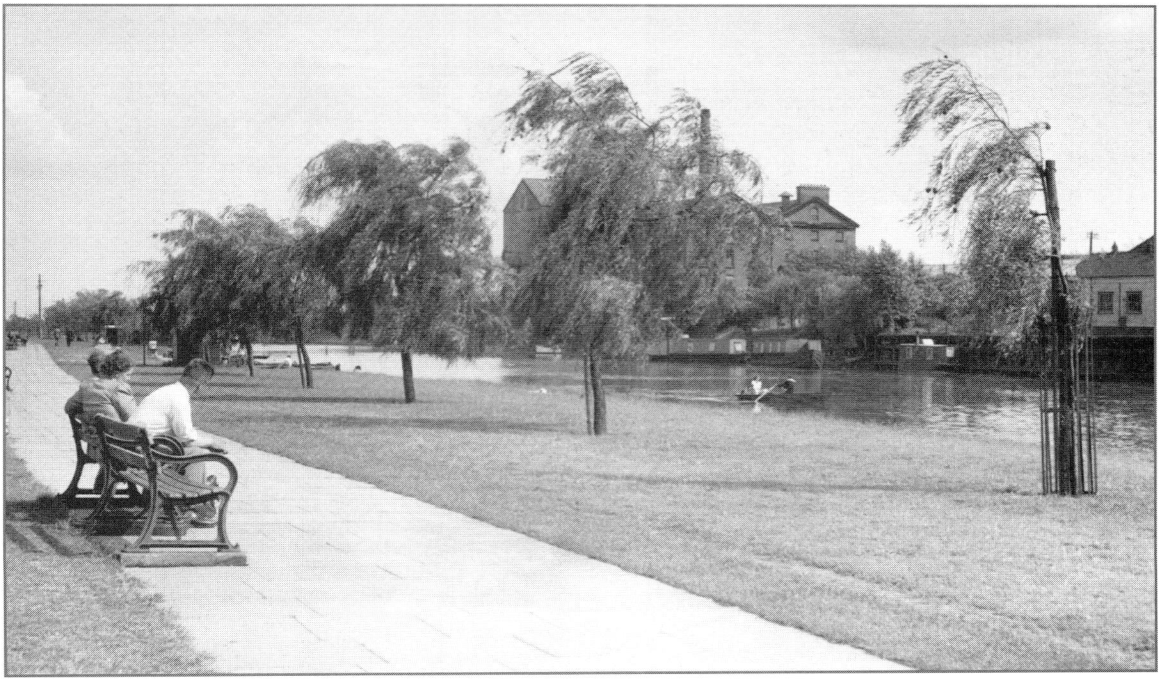

The River Embankment c1955 P47031

This photograph shows an ideal outlook for those with time to spare. Old industrial buildings and barges hint at the river's past industrial usefulness.

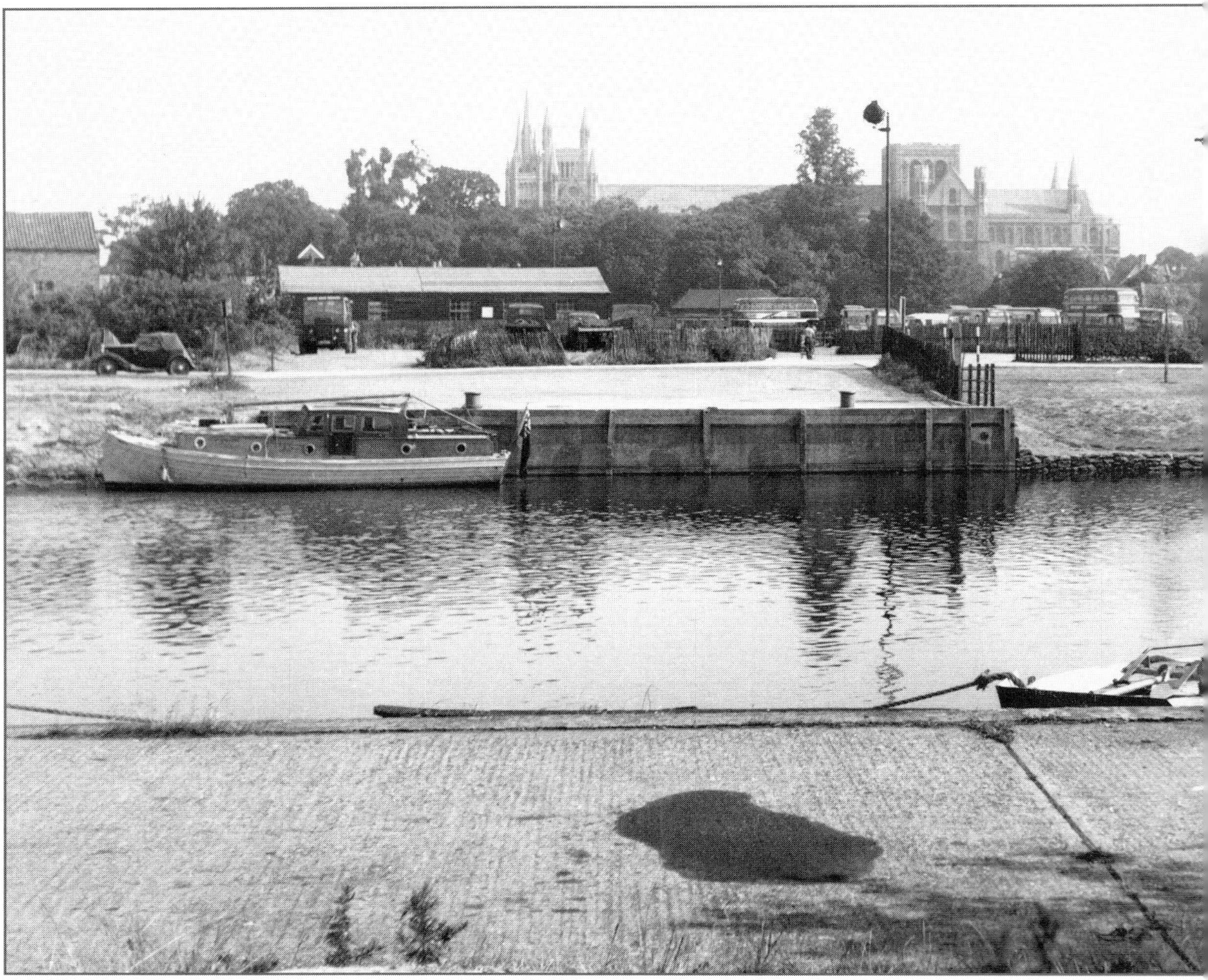

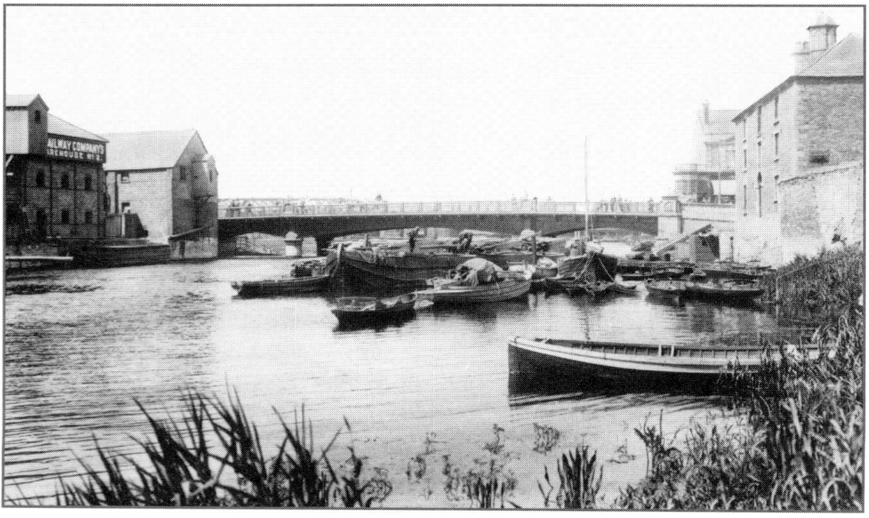

The Town Bridge 1904

51560

This photograph reveals the 1860 iron structure, and the business and bustle of a working port. The Nene valley has been important for Peterborough's development as a railway junction; there are complexes of lines and buildings, and the LNWR runs near the bank. Their No 2 goods warehouse is visible on the far left. The Customs House is far right.

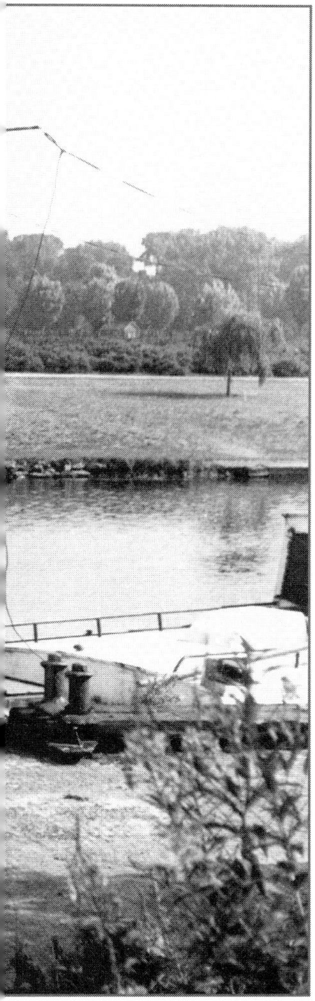

◄ **The River Nene c1955** P47034

We are looking north across the river toward Bishop's Road, conspicuous by its buses. A few lorries of the period are parked on rough ground behind a hut; this makes a contrast with the full south-east outline of St Peter's Cathedral. Leisure cruisers were luxury items when this picture was taken, and add a touch of elegance to the waterside.

▼ **The River Nene 1952** P47041

Here we see the attractive 1934 bridge with the power station rising up behind it. Peterborough's first Lighting Order was made in 1893, and the first power plant was in an old Catholic Church in Queen Street in 1900. The Customs House was handed over to Sea Cadets in 1942. There is a plethora of pleasure craft in view. The Patent Safety Ladder Co's premises off Oundle Street are just visible beyond the bridge.

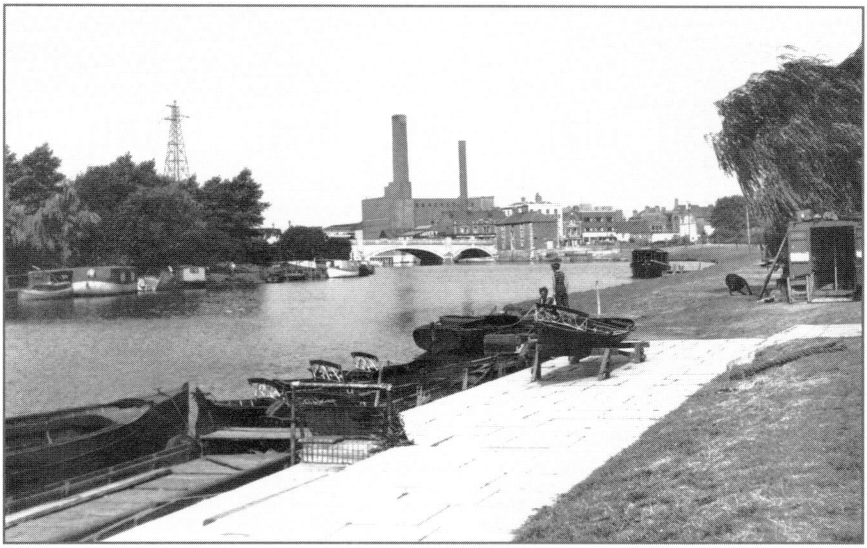

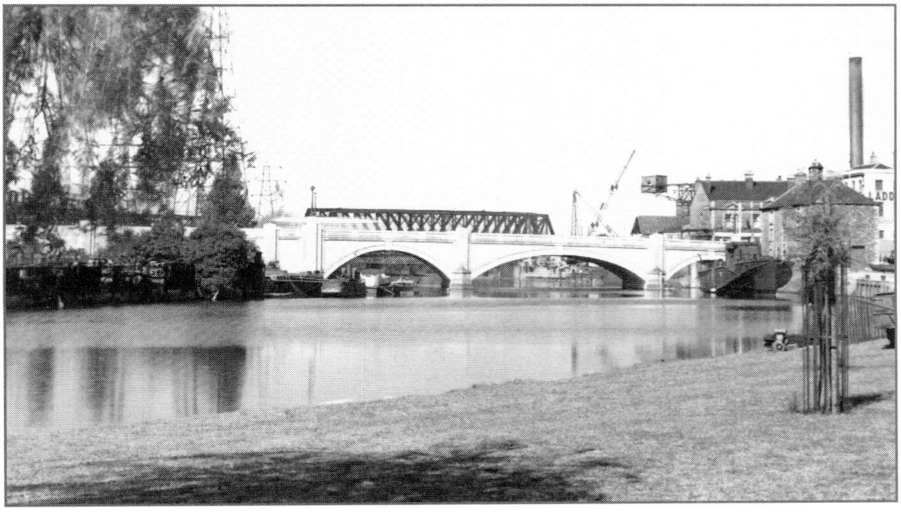

◄ **The Town Bridge c1955** P47006

This closer picture provides a clearer view of the power station operations. We can also see the railway bridge carrying the main line to London King's Cross, which links up with the Nene Valley route, and the Fletton brick sidings.

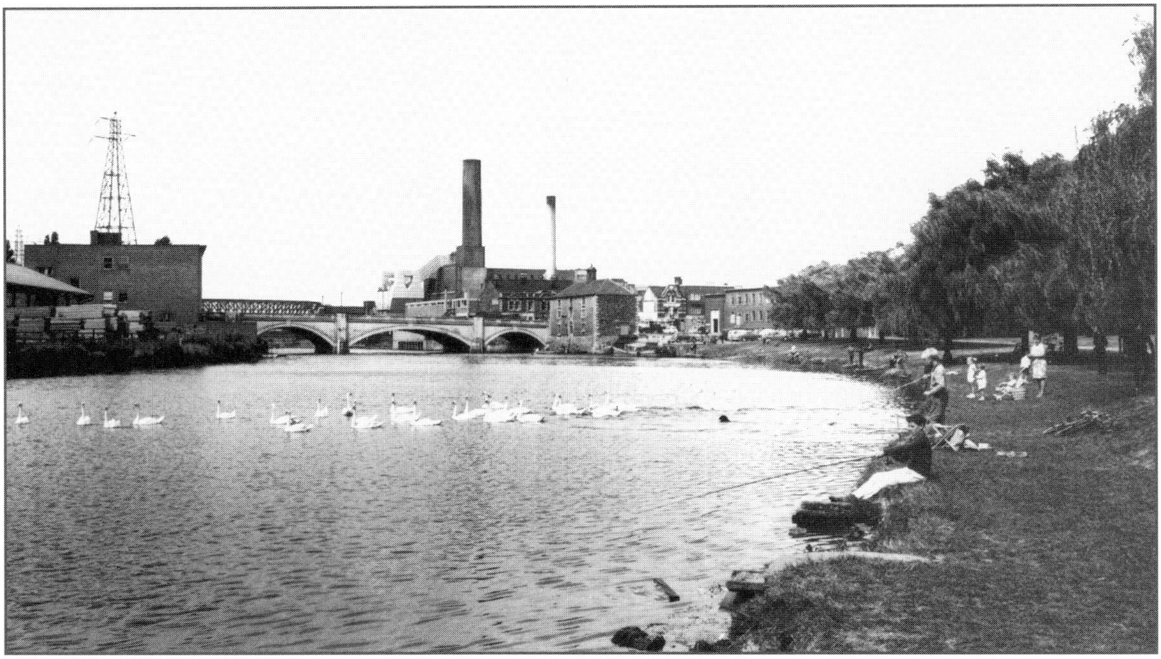

The River c1965 P47094
At this time many of the previous riverside features are still in place. Fishing seems to be a man and boy thing, while the lady and the younger children look on. The power station has centre stage, its 120-foot chimney making quite a landmark. But the life of this particular modern cathedral has not matched St Peter's, for it was demolished in 1978-80. Fortunately, the spot is just as popular with swans now as it was then.

The Fens

Hereward the Wake took refuge here after the Normans came, and before him St Guthlac, of Mercian royal blood, founded his hermitage at Crowland. A few miles away, Thorney, or the Isle of Thorns as it was, is about the flattest of fenland. It was an isolated island swamp when a handful of monks arrived in 662 to take on a hermit's life. One of them, named Tatwin, took St Guthlac to Crowland in 699. This early religious home was destroyed by the Danes in 870, and the abbey was re-founded for Benedictine monks in 972. The present church was built between 1089 and 1108; when the abbey was dissolved in 1539, the property was granted to the Earl of Bedford. A hundred years later, the incumbent Earl teamed up with the Dutch engineer Vermuyden to drain the fens, making village development like Thorney, Crowland and Whittlesey possible.

Drainage technology improved throughout the 1800s. Wind pumps were used to keep water levels down in an area that was gradually sinking as the peat dried out. The 19th-century steam age ►

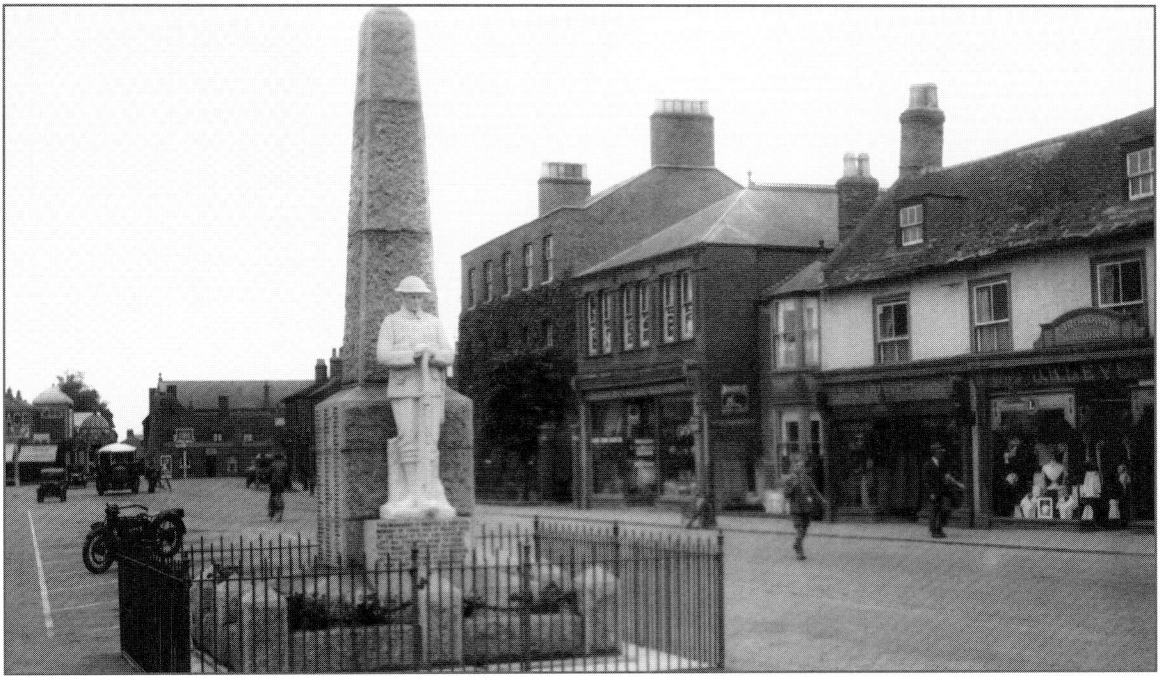

March, The War Memorial and Broad Street 1929 81906

Motor traffic is conspicuously lacking - a great contrast with today. J B Levett, Gents Outfitters, looks rather sober; one can imagine the serious chaps within, hierarchical, keen to serve, with tape measures at the ready. The local bus is parked in the background to ferry country dwellers to and fro. March is still a shopping centre, with a range of shops selling all sorts from ladies' flimsies to labourers' boots; it is on a busy coach route, served by National Express.

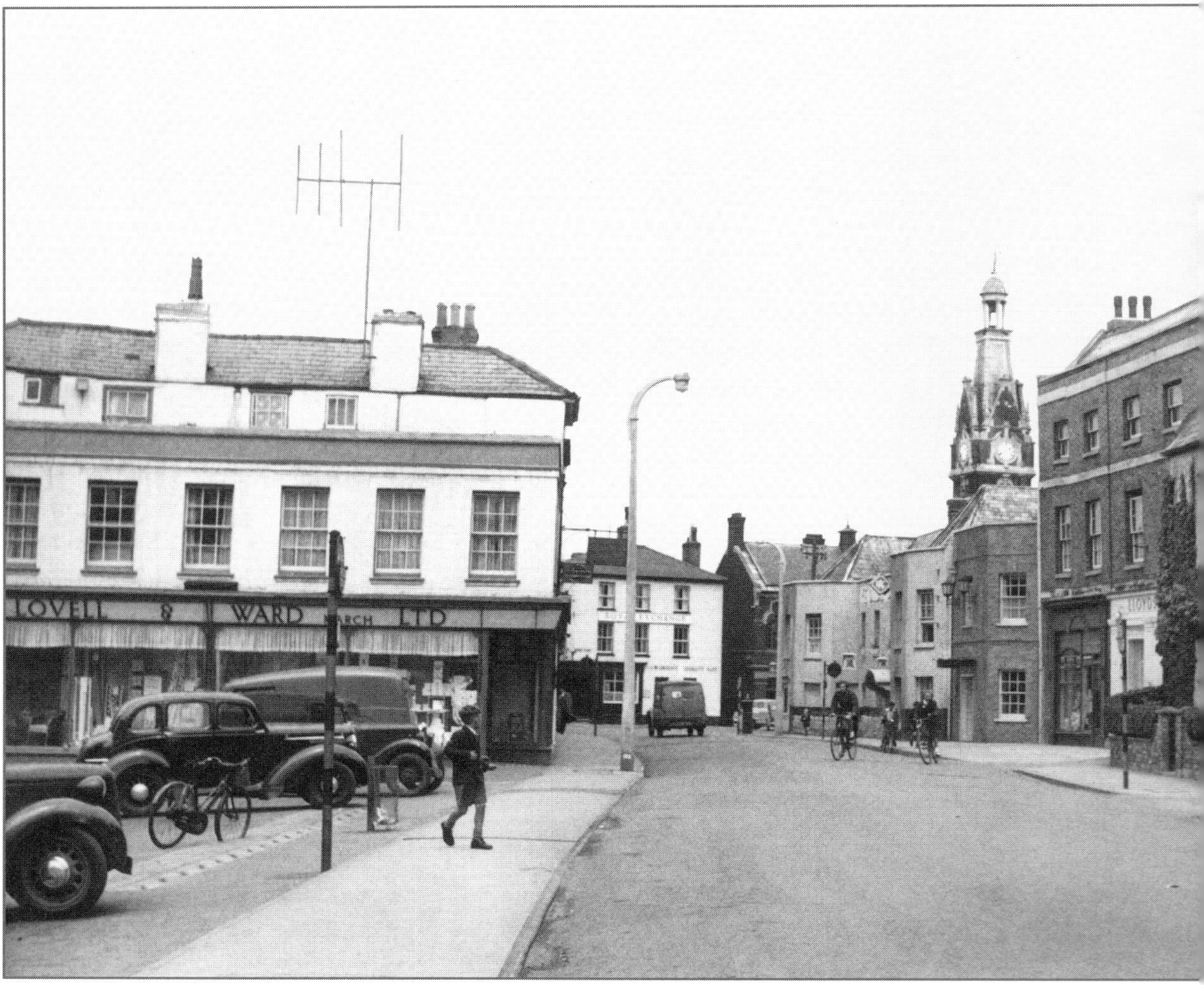

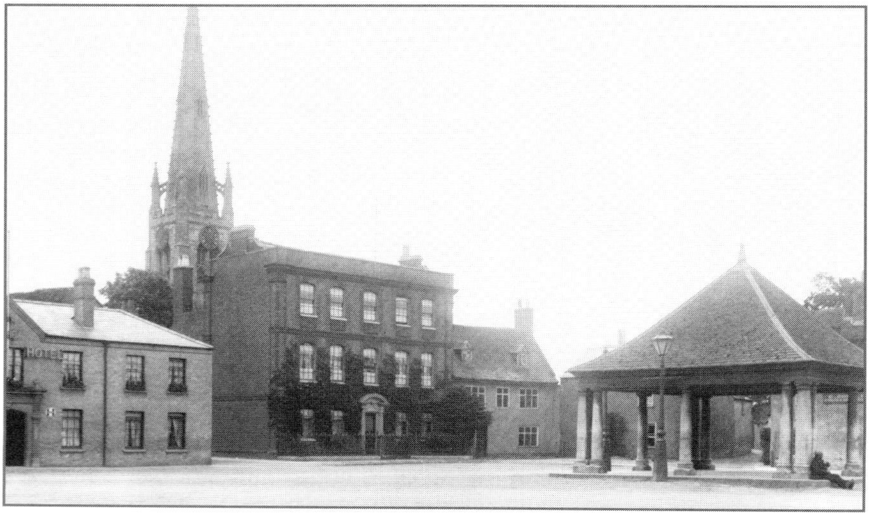

◀ **Whittlesey Market Place 1904** 51561
The Butter Cross is 17th-century. An old-timer reposes on the Butter Cross, looking rather lonely in this sombre setting. The beautiful vaulted spire of St Mary's sets off this grand little scene.

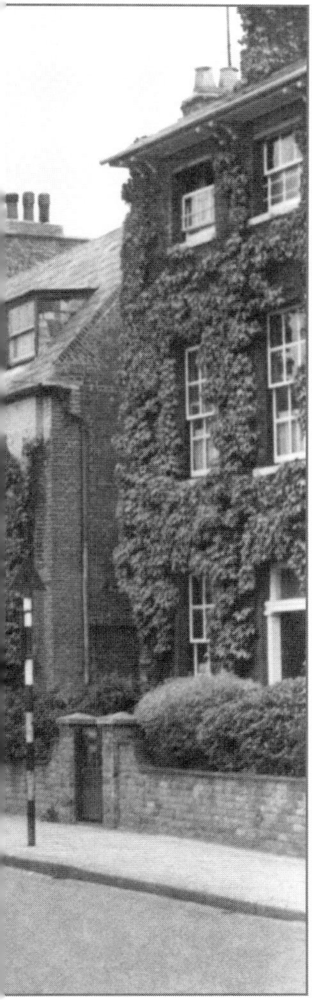

accelerated progress, and new centrifugal pumps replaced the mechanism of scoops mounted on giant wheels; tall engine houses stood out like pop-up pictures on the flat landscape. Rivers were straightened and new channels cut, improving drainage and expanding lengths of navigable water for the sake of trade and communication. By the end of the 19th century, today's modern landscape was established, productive in vegetables, fruit, flowers and cereals. With the railway connecting through March, the region's goods travelled swiftly. Alas, this saw the demise of thatch for roofing, as slate could now be imported easily; but peat digging survived until the turn of the century.

Today, agriculture struggles everywhere, though combines can still be seen kicking up plenty of dust at harvest, running under the gaunt pylons that straddle across the landscape like droopy-armed giants carrying heavy weights. Peter Westbrook turned to combine-driving when his job as a steam engine fireman went and Whitemoor marshalling yards closed down: 'I miss the big old steam engines and Whitemoor's a prison now. It used to assemble mixed goods traffic for Tilbury and Harwich. I came to March as a boy during the war, from London, went courting at the Hippodrome among other places, saw 'Gone with the Wind' there. It's all bingo there now'.

◀ **March, High Street c1955** M28036
There have been a few changes here, with the sombre RAC hotel today having made way for a paradoxically modern-sounding Ye Olde Griffin. Pre-war cars and boys in long shorts proclaim the 1950s, but the big 'H' looming up on the chimney pot above Lovell and Ward signals that television has arrived.

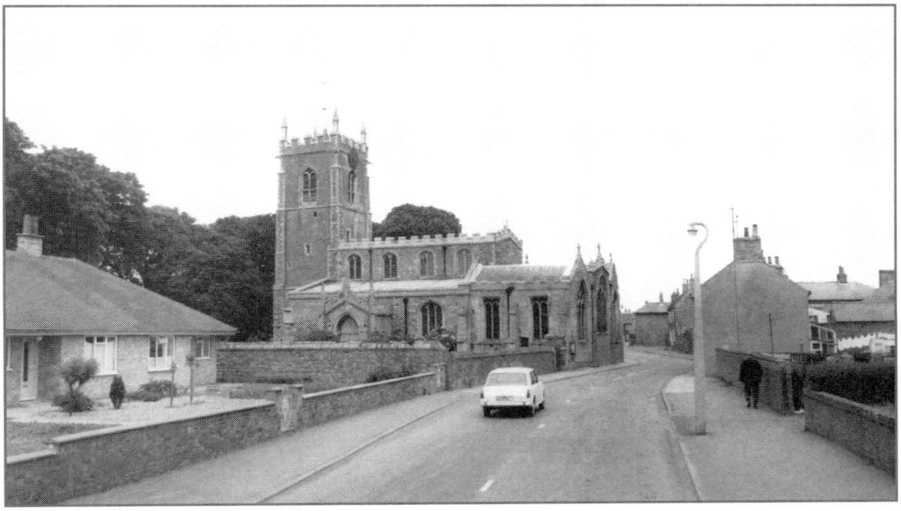

◀ **Whittlesey St Andrew's Church c1965** W90002
A neat little Morris 1100 passes a trim modern bungalow as it approaches the church, and judging by the packed clothes line it's Monday - wash day. This is very much fen country. The last major drainage scheme in 1851, using a centrifugal pump, banished much of the wild fowl, along with the fevers and rheumatics that troubled fenlanders.

Whittlesey, Market Place c1965 W90012
The war memorial reminds us that the town did its bit during the struggle for modern civilisation. Today, there is a bit more bustle than in this picture, with shops like Beddy Buys Textiles, Babes and Ladies and the Aga Shop setting a lively scene.

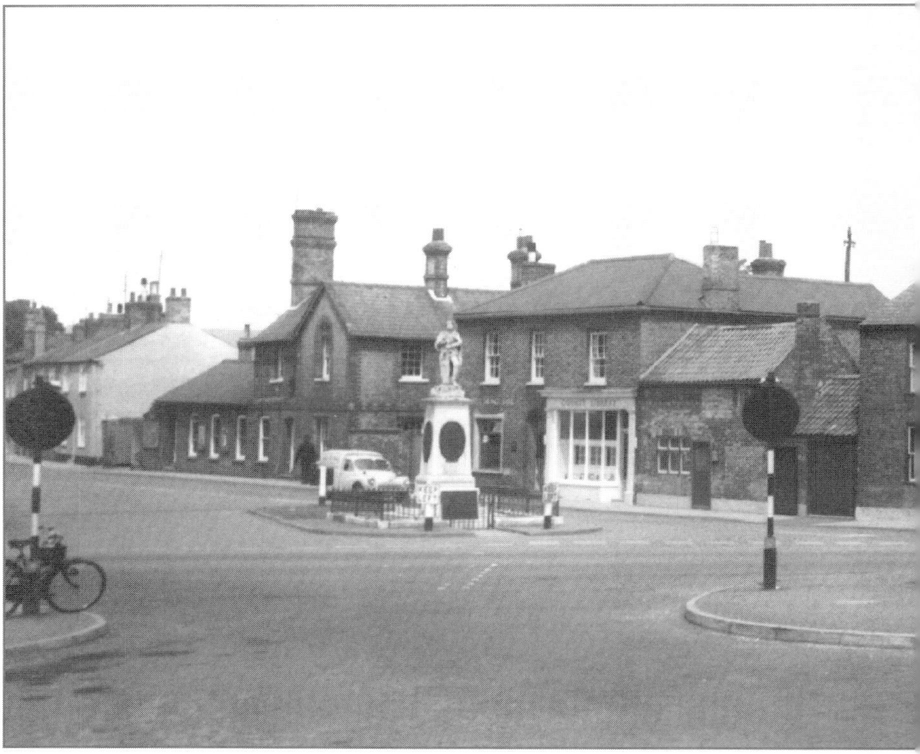

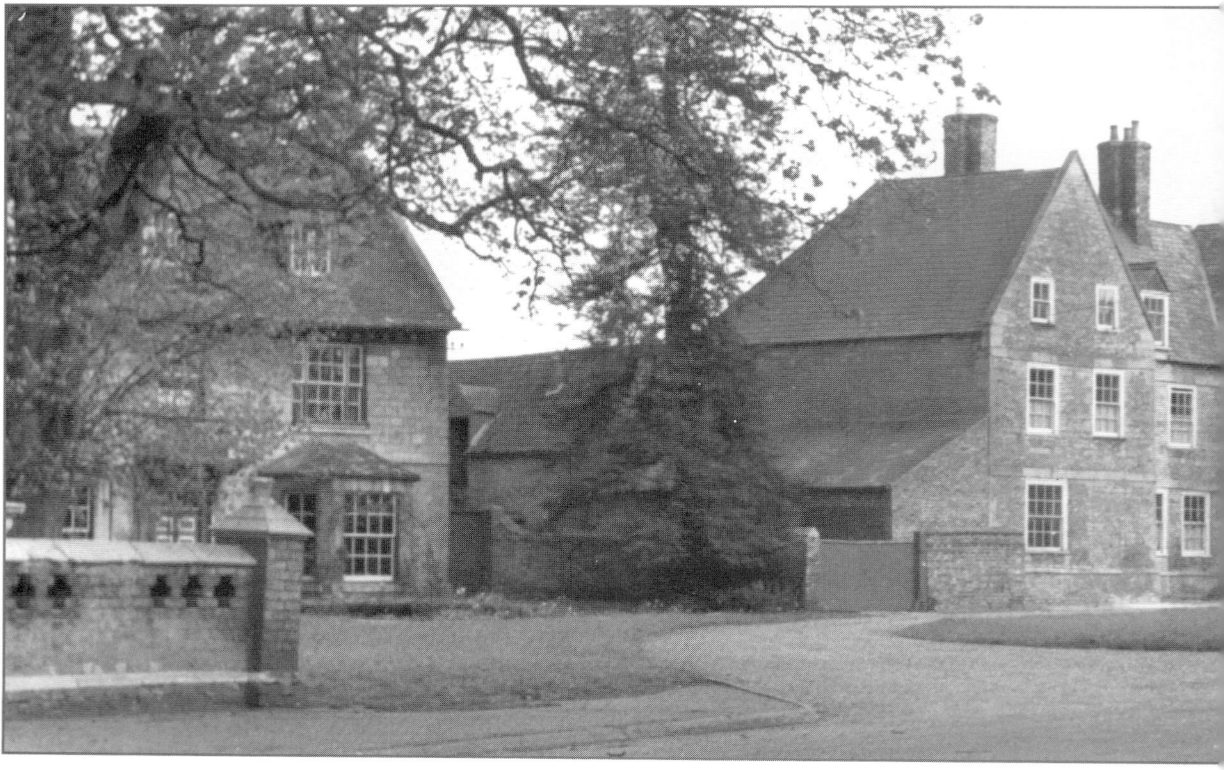

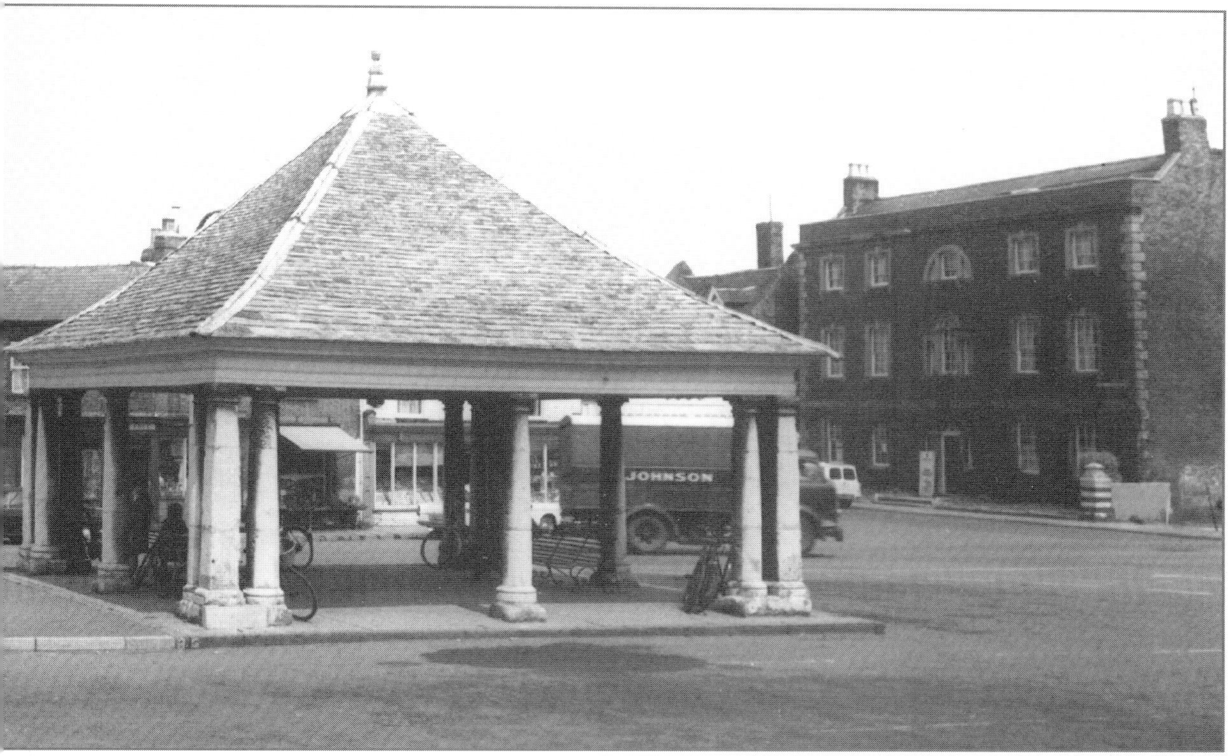

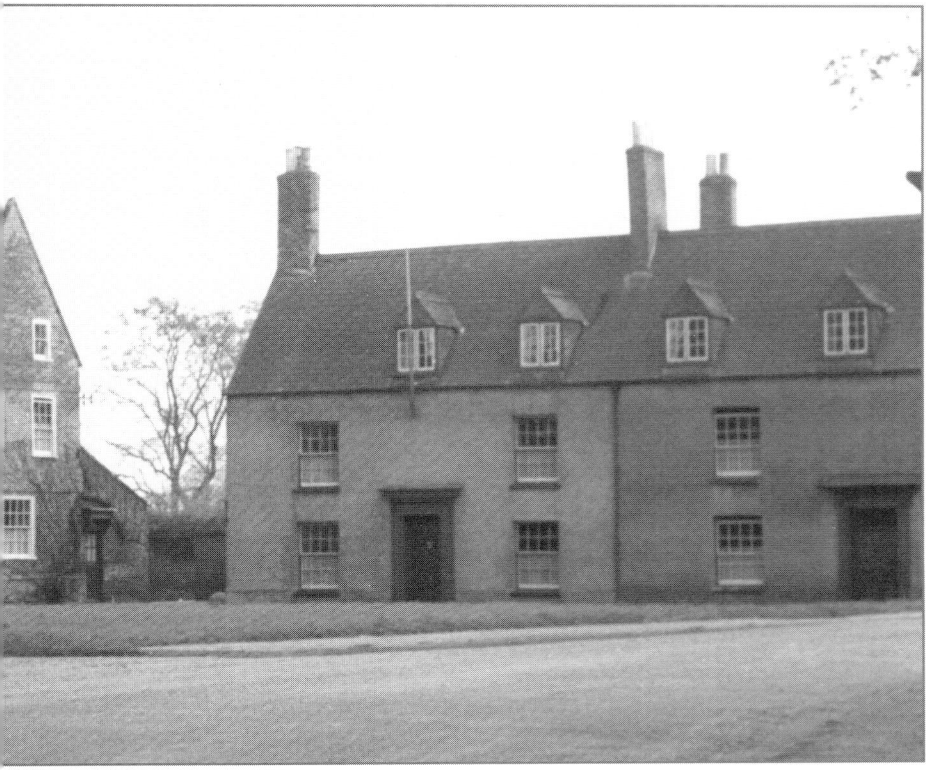

Thorney
The Village Green c1955 T33006
Looking much the same today, Thorney lies seven miles north-east of Peterborough on the busy A47 route to the east coast ports. The village eagerly awaits a relief road. It is hard to imagine a time when this was just a 7th-century settlement on the Isle of Thorns, or when Hereward the Wake hid in the marshes awaiting opportunity for revenge on the Normans.

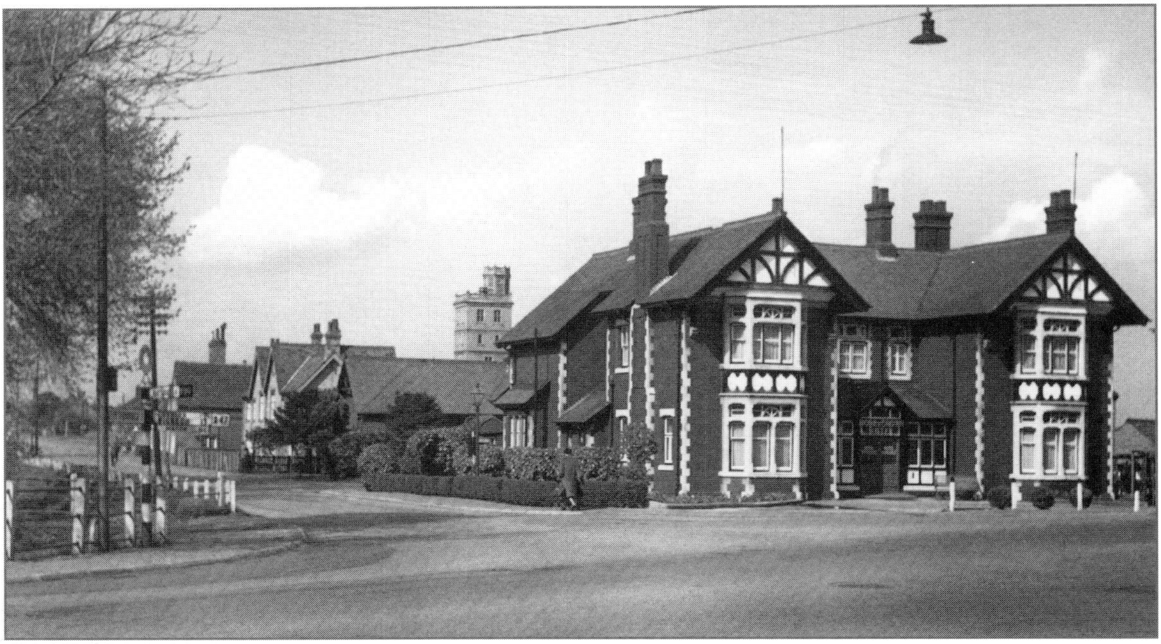

Thorney, The Rose and Crown Hotel c1955 T33005

Looking across the A47 for a clear view of the Rose and Crown like this would be almost impossible today; traffic lights are needed to clear the carriageway across the road to Crowland. This image predates commuters, juggernauts and the demise of the railways.

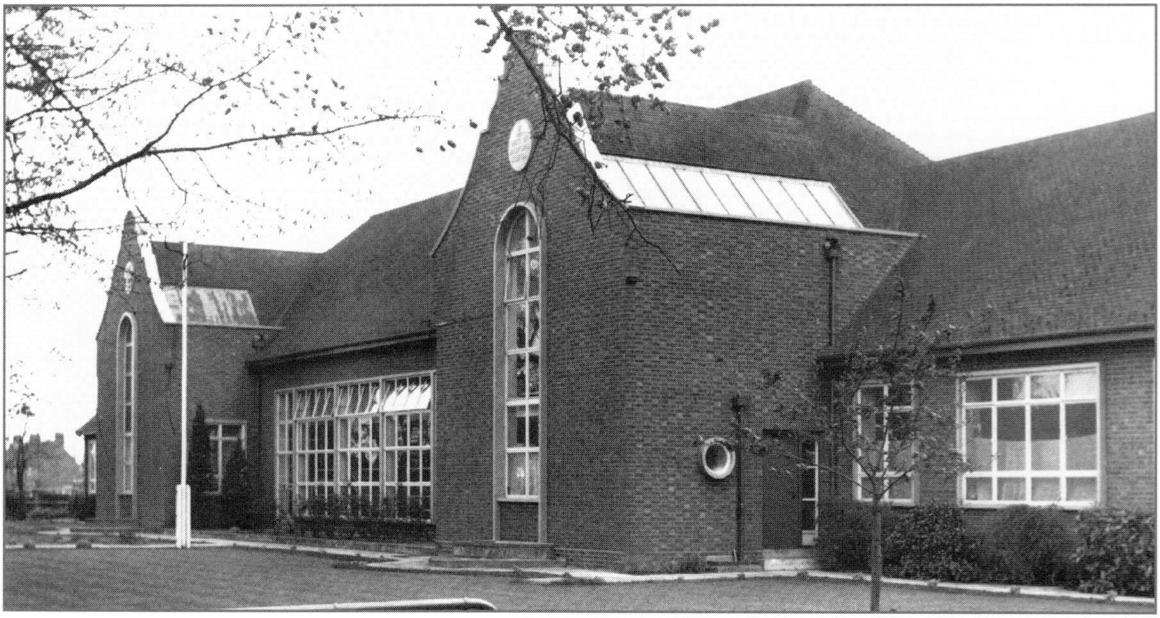

Thorney, Duke of Bedford School c1955 T33010

The name evokes the dukedom's historic link with the area. Records describe the local church in 1089 as a fragment of what it was. The abbey was dissolved in 1539, and the property was given to the Earl of Bedford. Partly demolishing it, he showed his enthusiasm for education by donating stone towards building Trinity and Corpus Christi Colleges, Cambridge. The school is a fitting reminder.

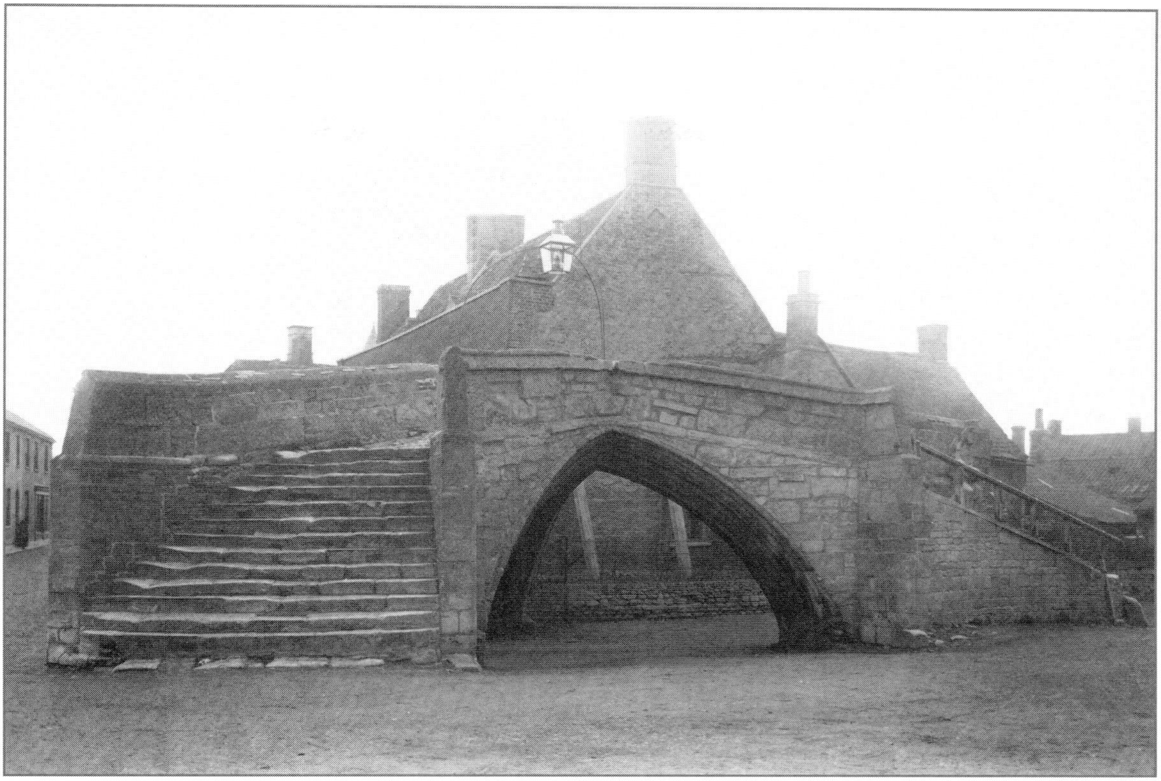

Crowland
The Bridge 1894 34833
Built of Ancaster limestone, the bridge replaced a wooden structure in the 14th century; it is not far from the ruined Abbey, which is said to have been founded by King Ethelbald in memory of St Guthlac. The abbey was burned by the Danes, rebuilt in c930, and burnt again in 1114, before being shaken by an earthquake. Crowland has been called eerie, and its history helps that image. The bridge is unique, with three arches meeting at 120 degrees and a carved seated figure: this was removed from the Abbey's west front, and is said to be of Christ or King Ethelbald.

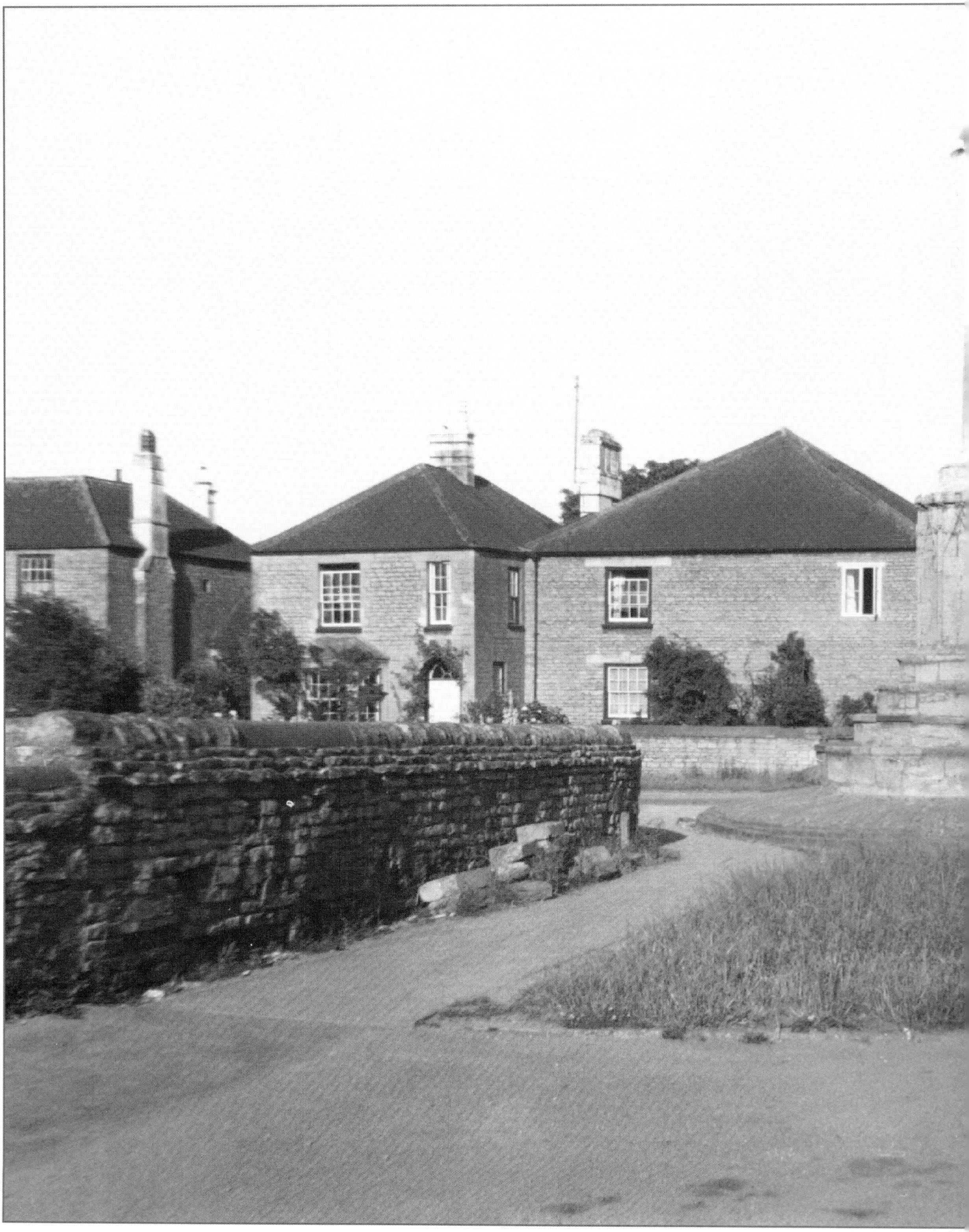

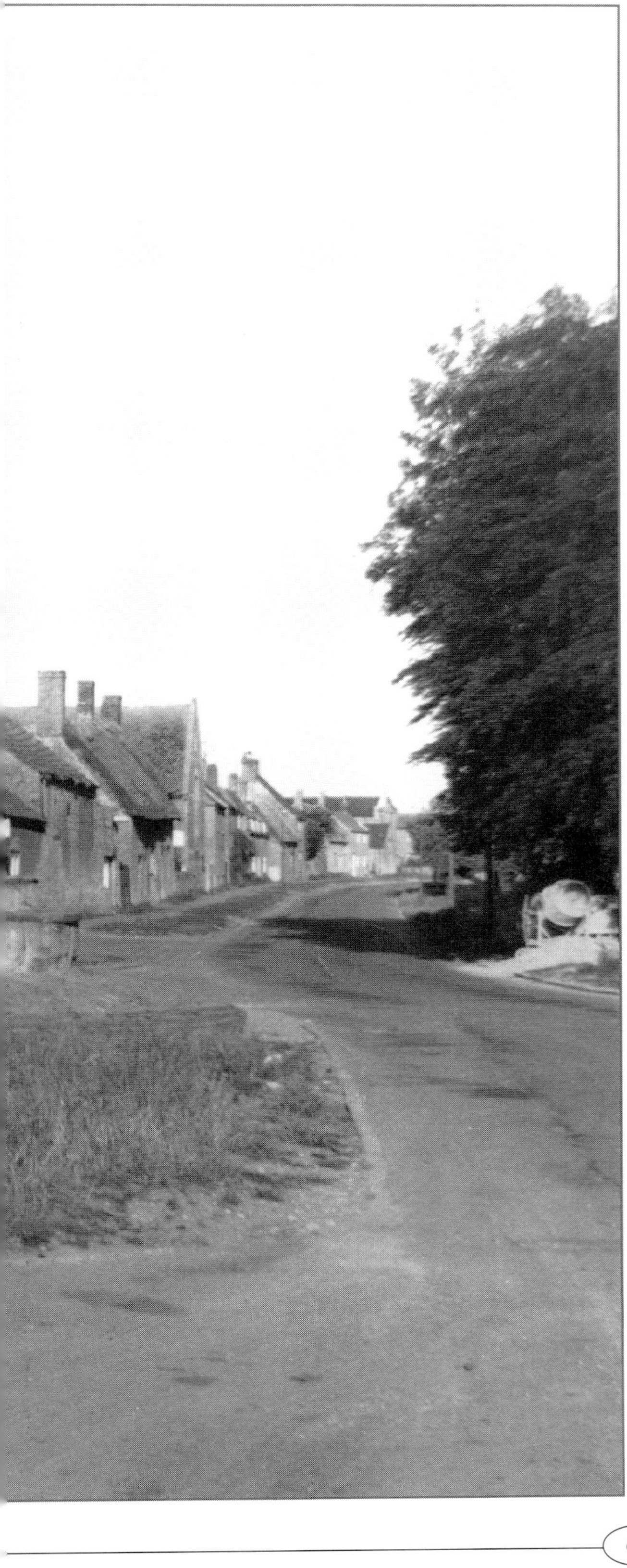

South & West

Agriculture flourished here during Roman times; the land was managed and drained with great efficiency. Castor had a healthy pottery industry, and Castor ware was exported to the northern empire. The Romans also discovered valuable iron and stone deposits, though there was no settlement this far north to equal Towcester on Watling Street.

Ordinary people saw little ease in their lives until the breakthroughs of the 20th century. Before that, it was a brave man or woman who stepped out of line. John Clare was an exception. Born in a roadside tenement on the edge of Deeping Fen, he minded horses, did odd jobs, learned his letters, picked up Thomson's 'Seasons' and began to write verses. At Helpston, his family lived in a ►

Helpston, The Cross c1955 H434002
This Northamptonshire village is the birthplace of the rustic labourer poet John Clare, 1793-1864. A cross was erected in his memory and he was buried in the local churchyard, which is to the right of this scene.

quarter of 'a narrow hut in a plain covered with stagnant pools and overhung by mists'. He compared it to a cave. His art was to suggest the tiny detail of nature, but his sensitivity proved a weakness. In better days he would take the weekly river packet to March, or watch surveyors plan a railway line. Toward the end of his life, he sat on a bench outside All Saints Church in Northampton, gazing blankly. In the end he faced Northampton's asylum. Perhaps the raw beauty of his native landscape overwhelmed him. Upon the matter of the Enclosure Act he wrote:

'It levelled every bush and tree
And levelled every hill,
And hung the moles for traitors
Though the brook is running still;
It runs a naked stream cold and chill'.

Rural change has been relentless and dramatic, making dormitory towns of places like Castor and Ailsworth, but strong features of rural past and beauty remain. Stilton evokes memories of a cheese-making tradition through the name of a local inn called the Stilton Cheese. Nowadays, Stilton's wide High Street looks out of place, but it used to serve as part of the A1. With the by-pass there is something of a time-warp atmosphere, and a tiny post office and a red telephone box complete the picture; though smart ladies walking labradors betray today's commuter link, and Lover's Lane just off the by-pass beckons the youthful or naughtier locals to enjoy certain timeless pleasures!

At the furthest point of this journey south of Peterborough there is Oundle, complete with its own new developments, but still very much its old self. Oundle is an old British name, like the River Nene upon whose banks it stands. Northamptonshire was part of outer Mercia, and the Eight Hundreds of Oundle was a federation of kin groups centred here. There was also a monastic settlement. The town prospered during the 10th century, with more land going to the plough. It was here that Aethelwold came after a vision revealed to him that St Peter's monastery was destroyed. He went on by river to begin rebuilding it.

Today Oundle's stone buildings shine gold and yellow in the sunshine, making a bright screen for following your shadow. Giggling schoolgirls move in packs like characters from 'Bunty' in the 1960s; their male counterparts at the well-known public school move more usually in twos, blazers flapping, deep in conversation, confident and assured. Ladies of leisure park expensive sports cars by the kerb to pop into the post office or curio shop, untroubled by traffic wardens. All is delightfully olde worlde, and so in keeping with a part of England that is still very much alive.

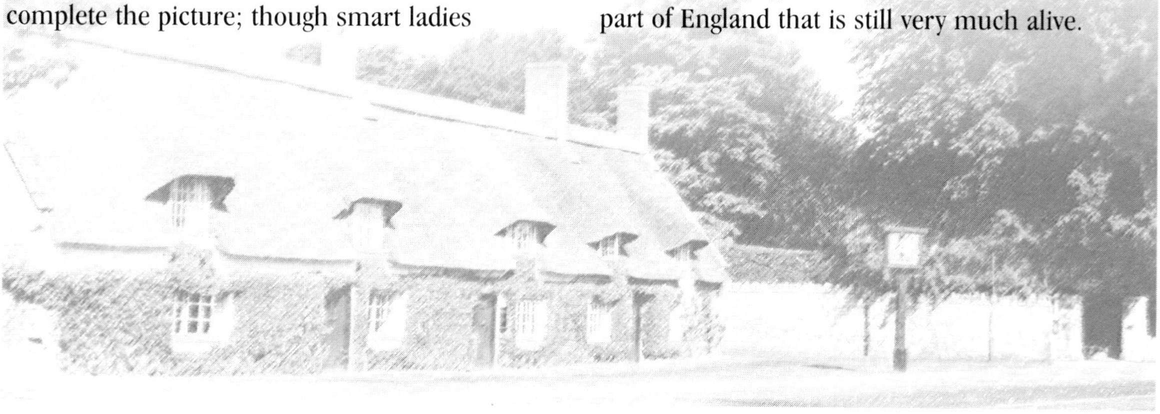

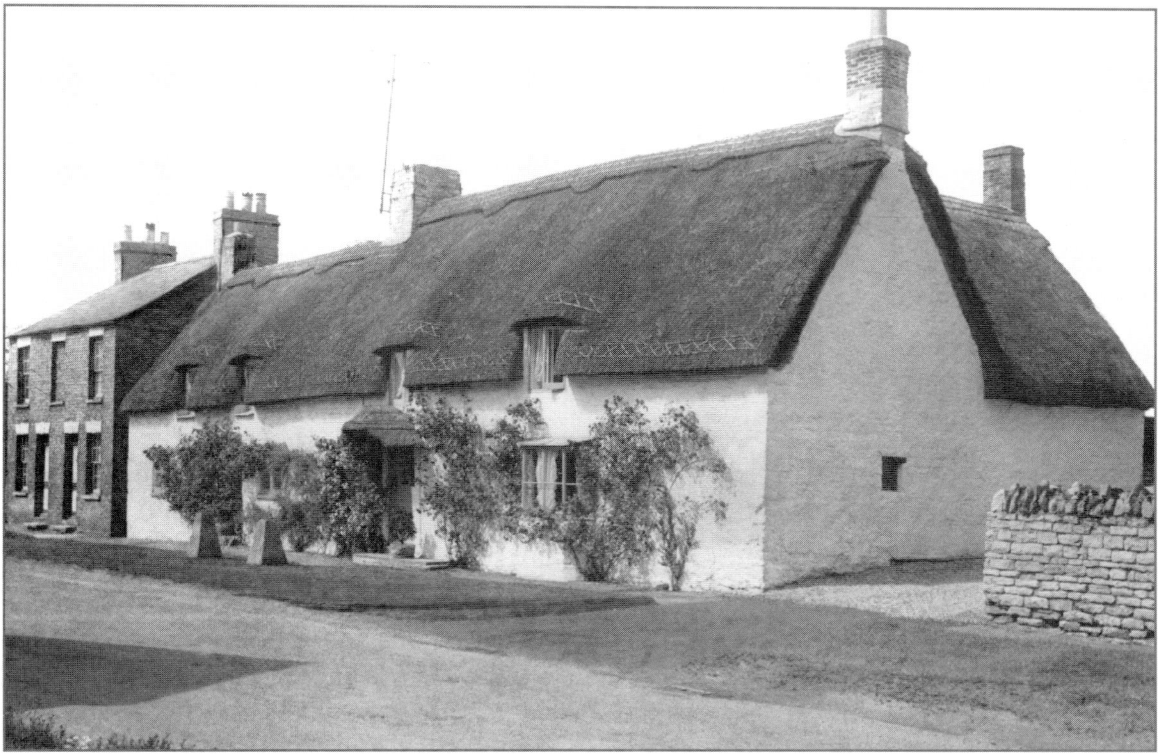

Helpston
Clare's Cottage c1955 H434006
John Clare's unhappy love for Mary Joyce and his final years in Northampton Asylum are part of his pathetic story. He lamented leaving his old home: he missed chiefly 'its yellow furze, molehills and rabbit tracks that lead through besom, lin and teasel burrs'.

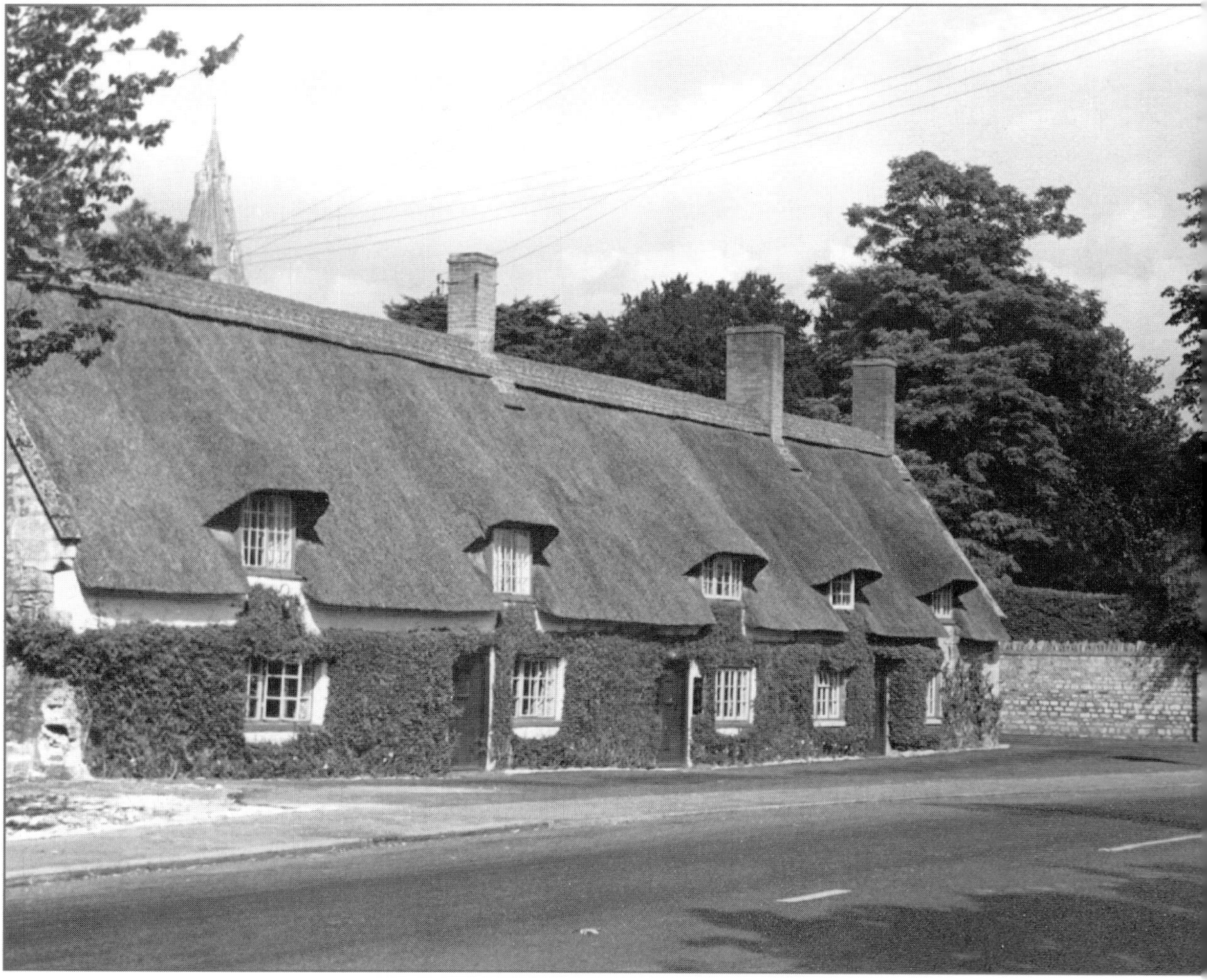

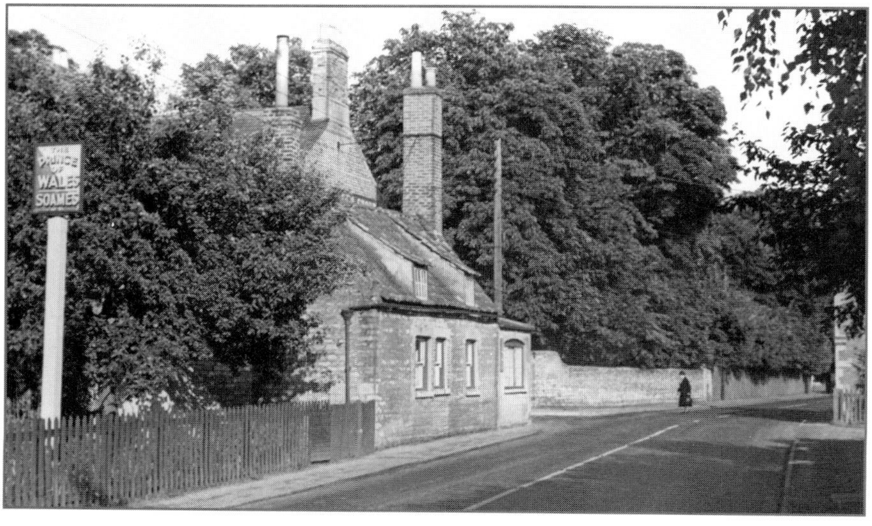

Castor, Main Road c1955 C584004

Here we see the use of local stone for building. The Prince of Wales is a name chosen to honour many pubs, and is fitting for a Royal County. But alas, the name is lost; the pub is now the Feathers, and the road outside it has had a chicane installed to calm the hurrying motorists.

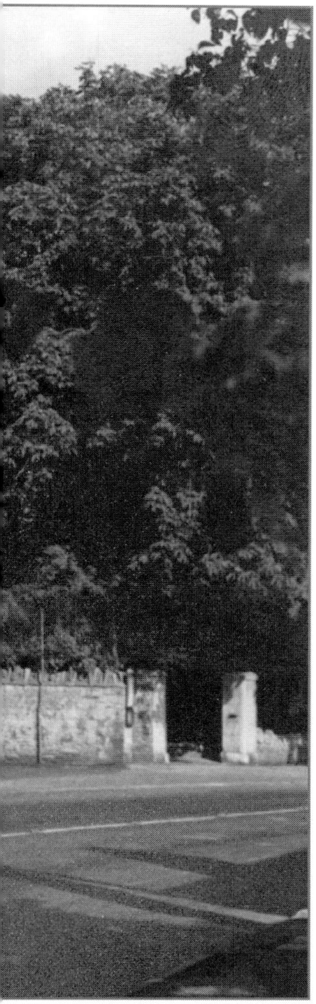

Castor, The Fitzwilliam Arms c1955 C584014
Castor and Ailsworth make virtually one affluent suburb of the city of Peterborough. The Fitzwilliam Arms evokes the name of old aristocracy, and fits in with the modern ambience. These days customers can sit outside on a summer's evening to unwind from executive stress in the fairy-lighted glow.

Stilton, High Street c1955 S673011
Historically the Great North Road made Stilton a busy place, though here in the 1950s it looks rather quiet. A huge Bell sign marks the ancient stone inn. The Stamford coach called here; it cost 4d (old pennies) a mile and a shilling to the coachman, and to send a letter cost 6d to 9d a sheet.

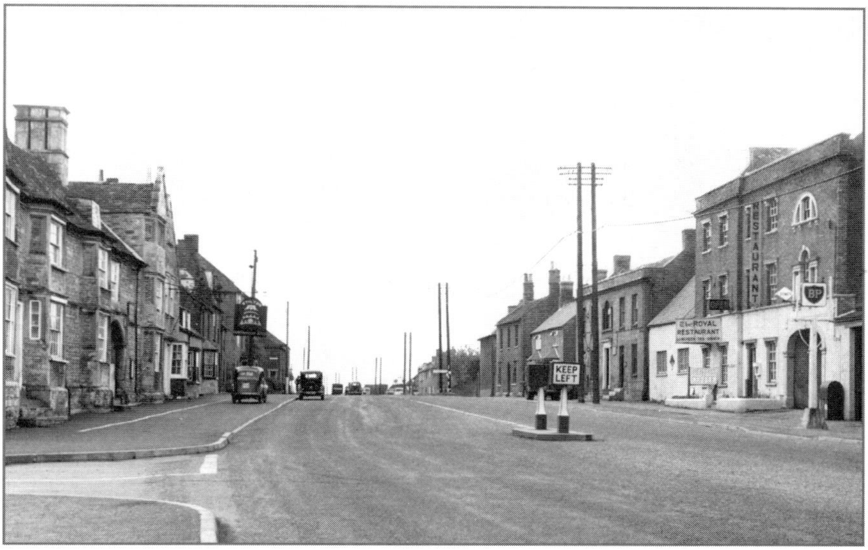

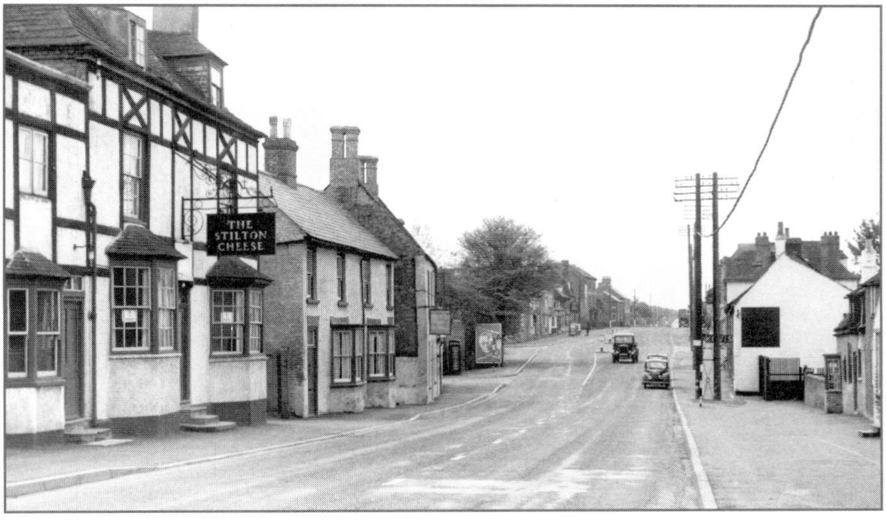

Stilton, High Street c1955 S673019
The High Street saw a lot of lorries, but at the time of this photograph they were a sensible size. This lorry coming will not shake old buildings like the Stilton Cheese. Stilton, a Huntingdonshire village, was a collection point for Stilton Cheeses made in Melton Mowbray. Note also the roadside billboard and the stately telegraph poles - this was definitely not the mobile phone age.

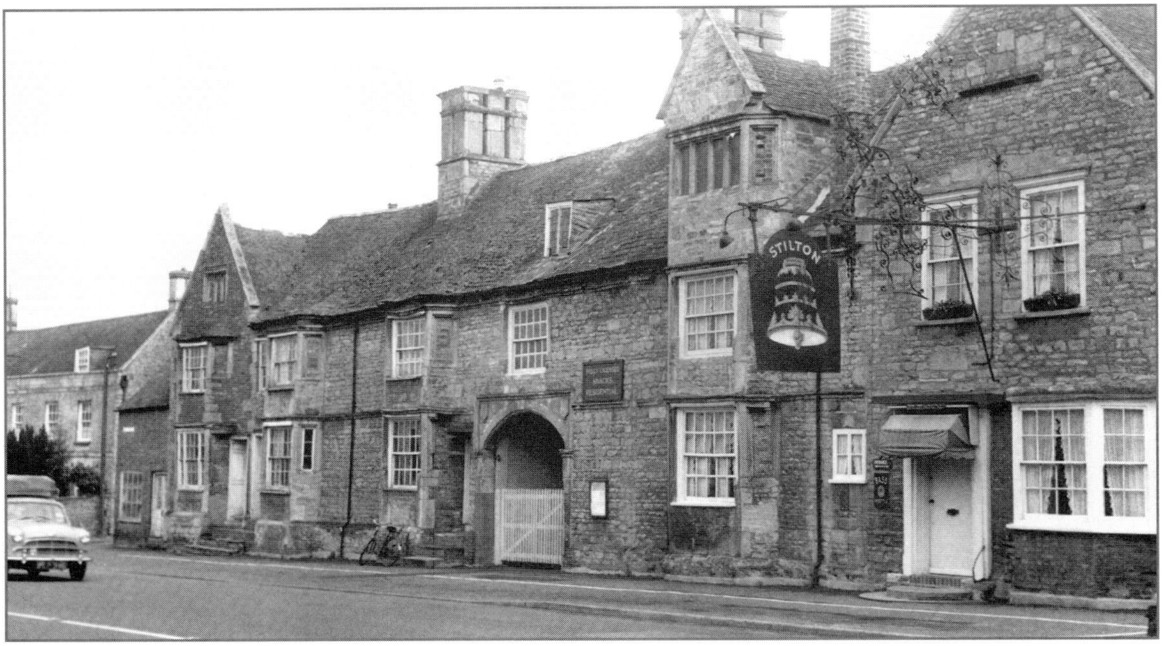

Stilton, The Bell Hotel c1965 S673020

The stone built Bell Inn, dating from 1642, is where Stilton cheeses were originally collected from Leicestershire villages; it also served the coach travellers on the Great North Road, which now bypasses the village. At the time of this picture, the A1 was a popular route.

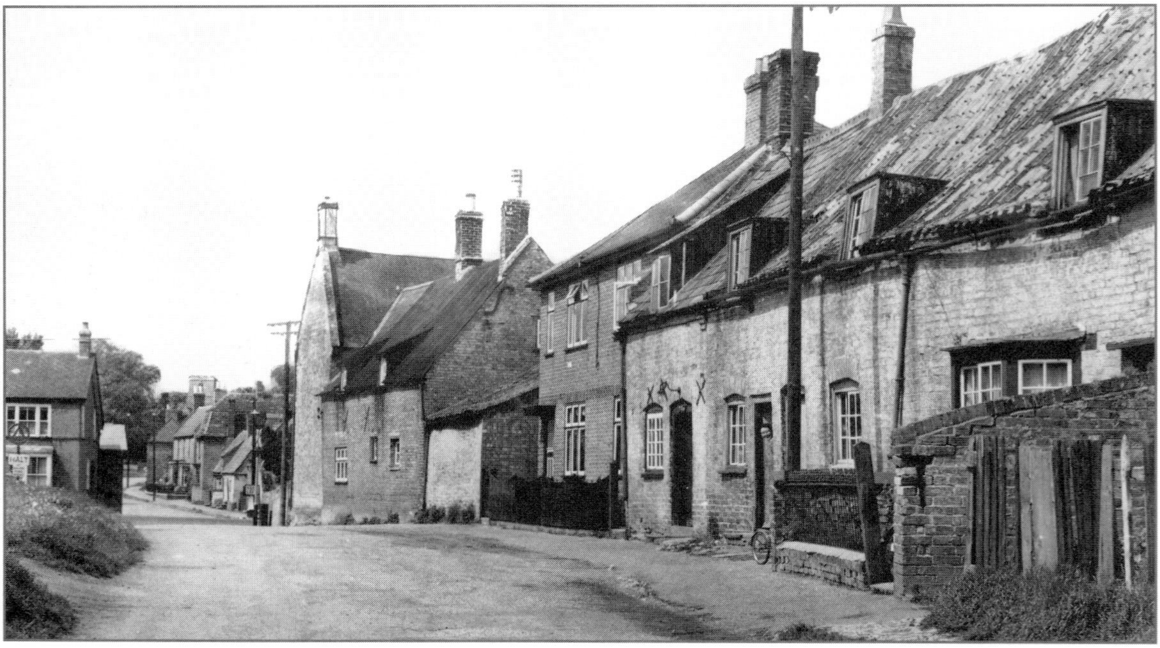

Stilton, Fen Street c1955 S673004

Stilton is a great place for antique buildings, including an Early English church with several brasses. Here is Fen Street all rustic in summer, with a happy-faced lady smiling at the photographer. I doubt if she had many amenities in that little cottage. TV aerials are absent: this was still the radio age, and television was a crude and expensive luxury.

Stilton, The Air Force Memorial
Norman Cross

Norman Cross Air Force Memorial is set in a wild exposed piece of landscape; it is there 'lest we forget' the British and American Air Forces stationed around these parts, who did their bit for our freedom.

Oundle
Market Place c1955

As it is built on the stone belt, this looks more like the Cotswolds. We can feel the gentle energy here. The little Ford van is advertising Automatic Electrical Refrigerators and has come all the way from Bedford. The Rose and Crown looks welcoming; the shop fronts hide under yards of white tent-like canopies, and the shadow tells us the time of day.

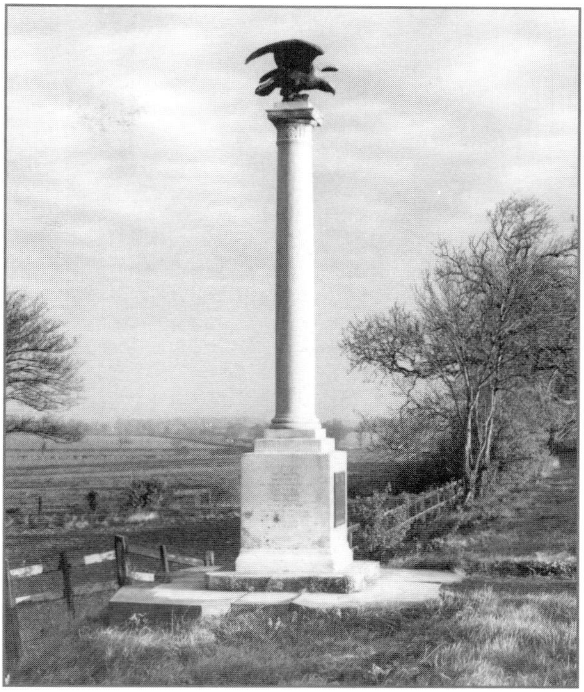

Stilton, The Air Force Memorial, Norman Cross
S673024

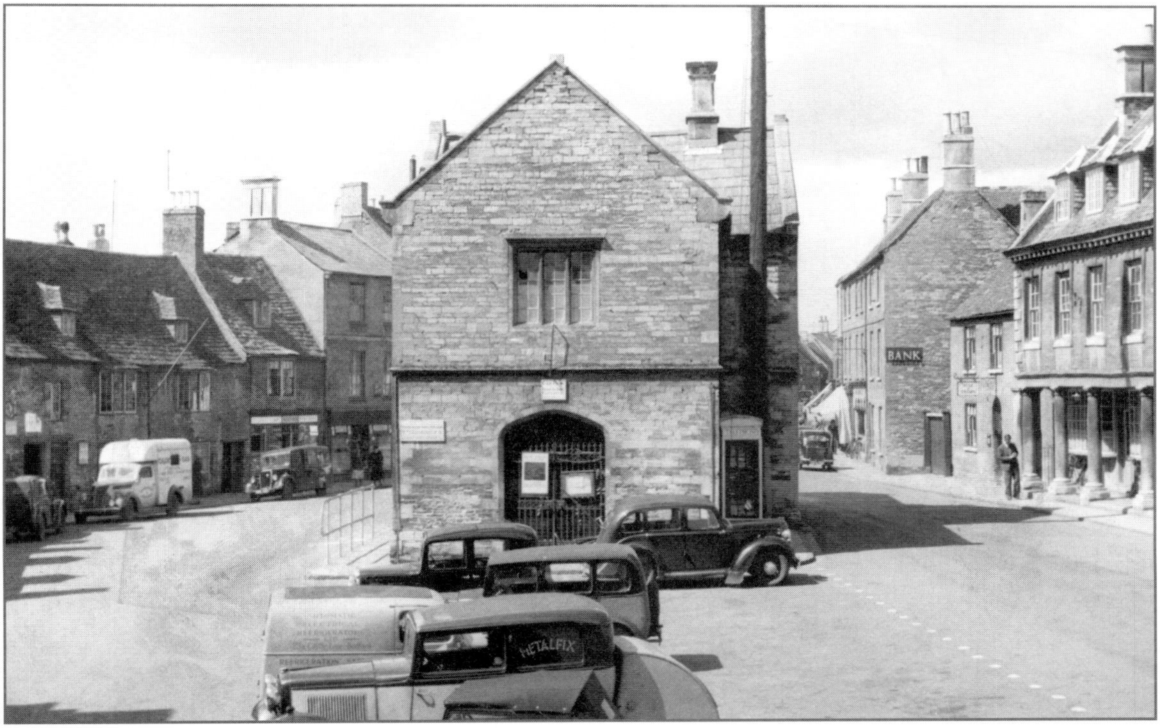

Oundle, Market Place c1955 O103033

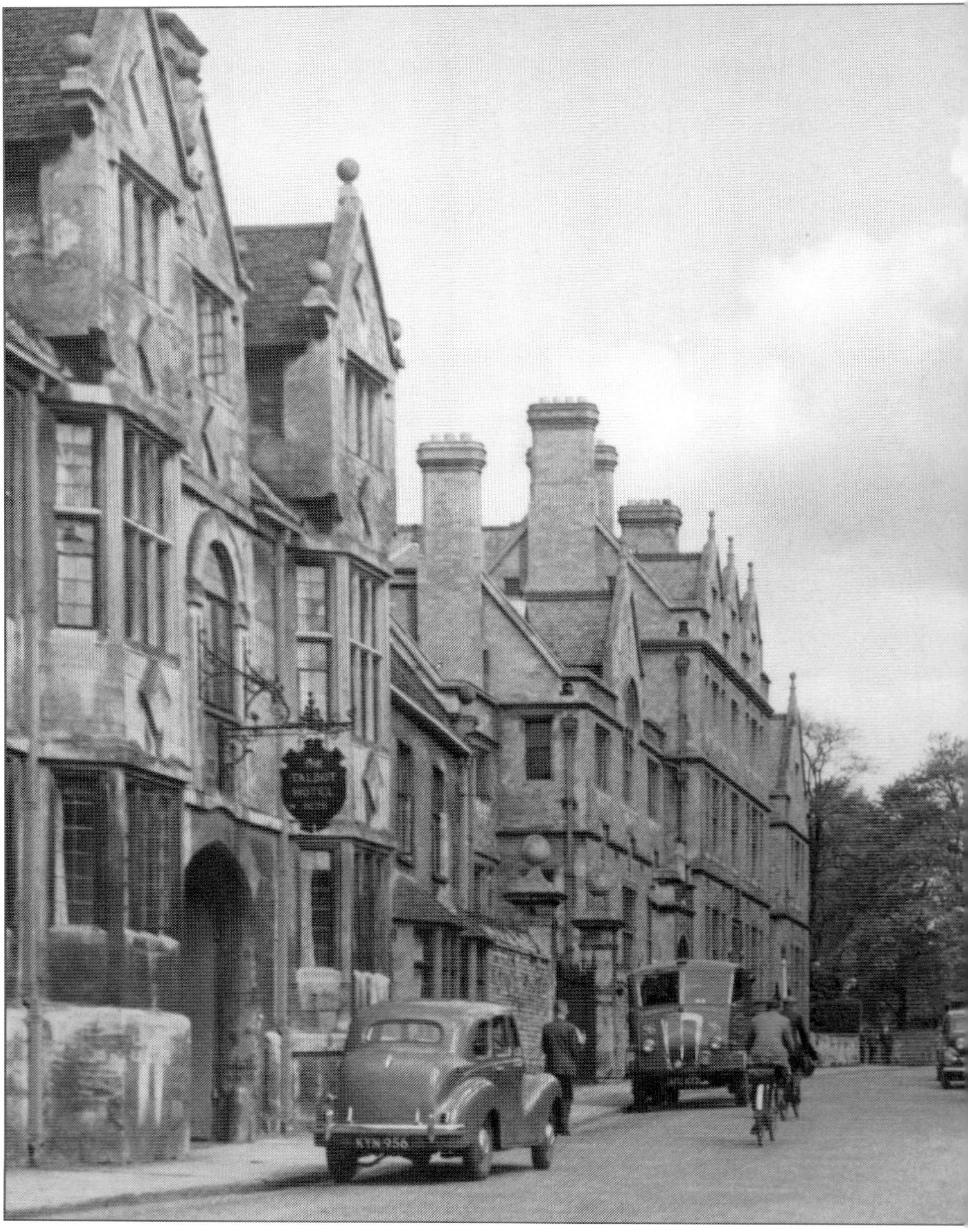
THE
TALBOT
HOTEL

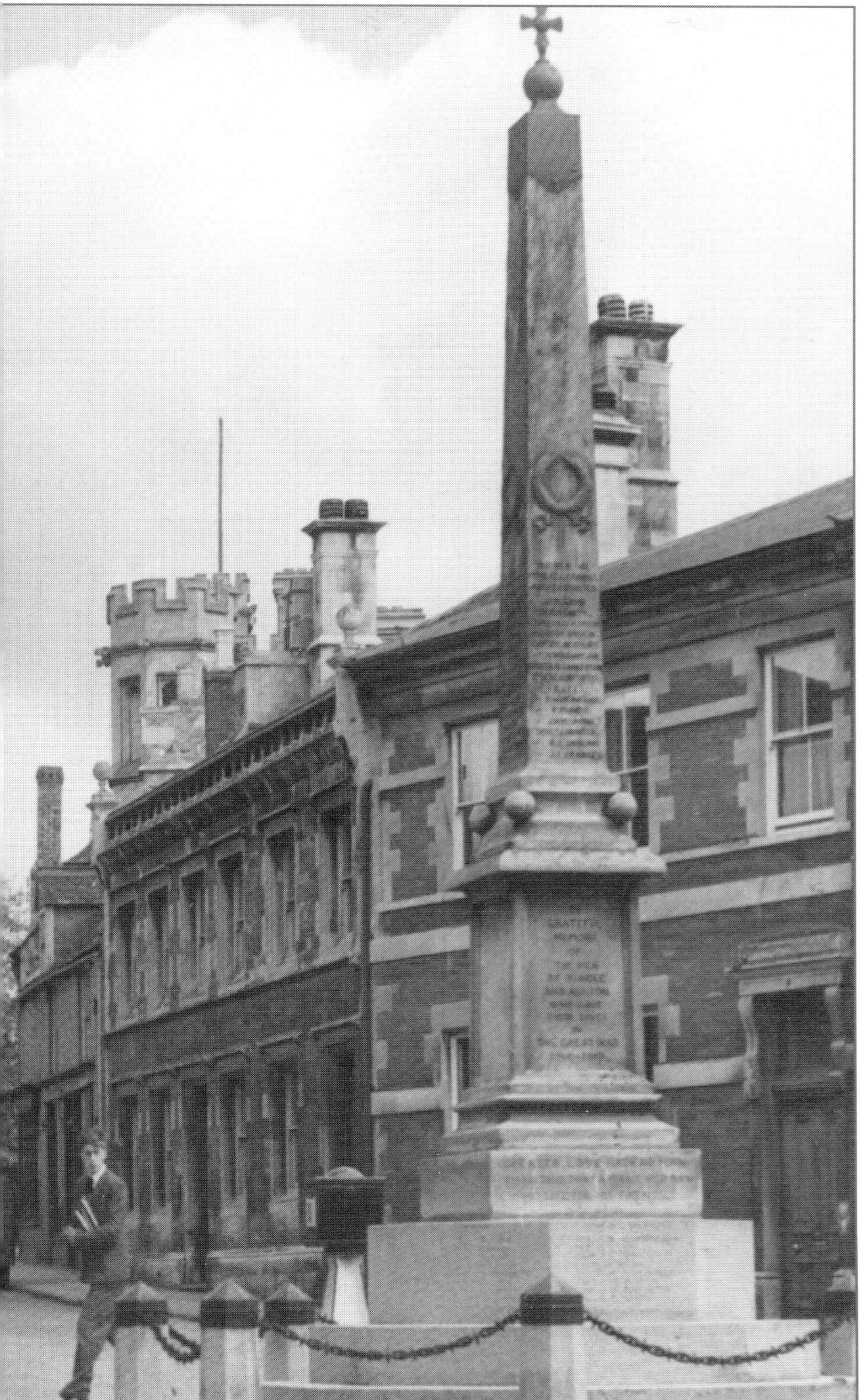

Oundle, New Street c1955 O103029
This view shows some of the town's best architecture, including the picturesque Talbot Hotel on the left. There is also a fine Early English church with a lofty crocketed spire and a beautiful south porch. In this scene there is a reminder of the studious tradition with a schoolboy walking purposefully behind the war memorial. I wonder what he is doing now!

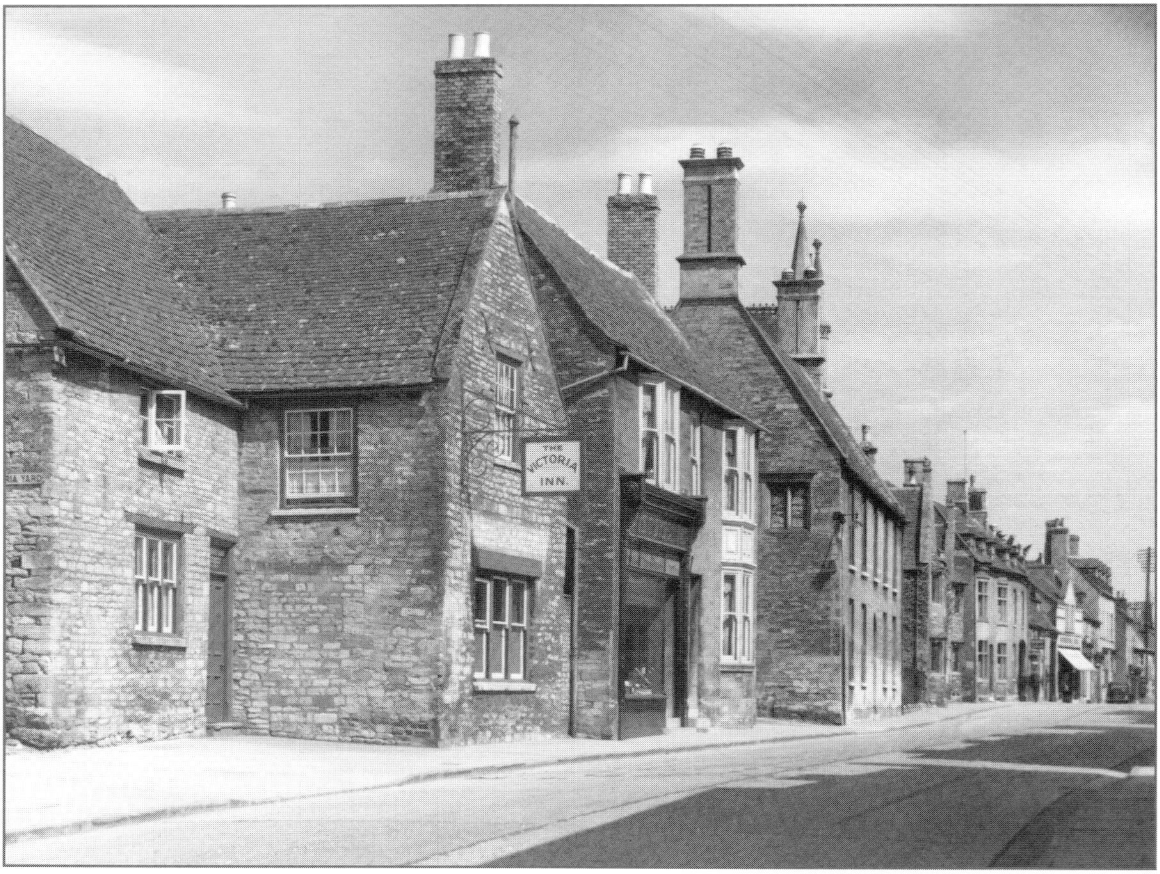

Oundle, West Street c1955 O103003
Here we see the consistency of style and architecture on this belt of Jurassic limestone. The Victoria Inn has gone, as have so many pubs; there are too many rival entertainments here, like the New Yang Tze River Chinese take-away. This is a town of elegant housewives and business suits, with culture on hand at the Rodolphe Stable Theatre.

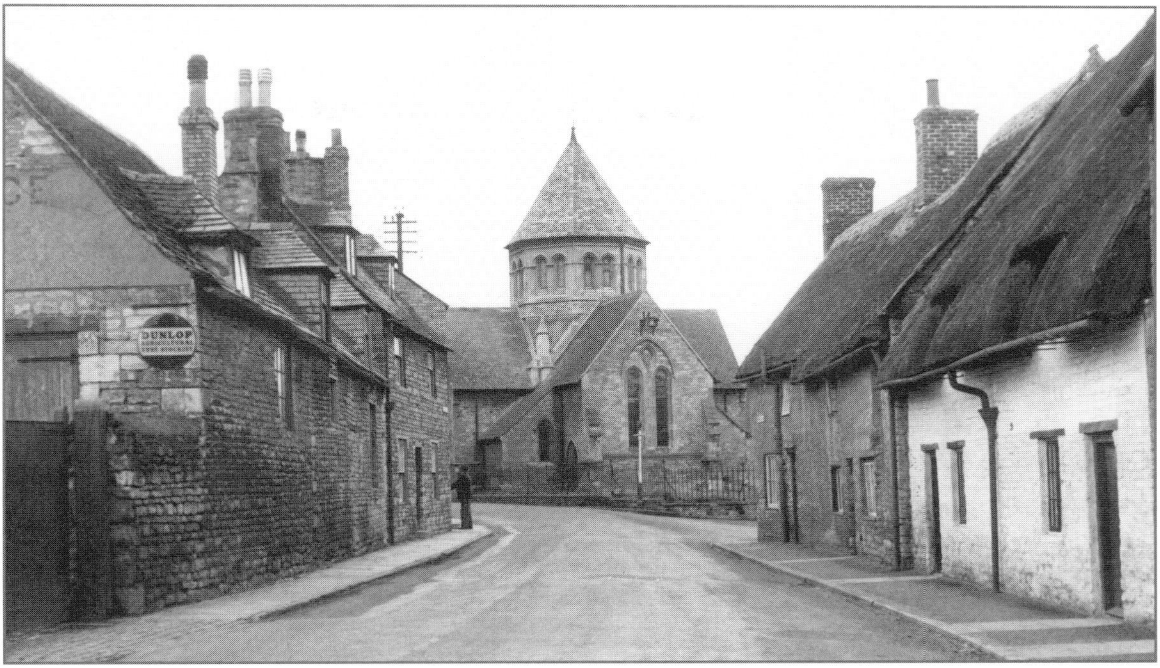

Oundle, Benefield Road c1955 O103024
We are looking toward Stoke Hill. The barn on the left advertises Dunlop Agricultural Tyres, reminding us that Oundle is in the heart of Northamptonshire farmland.

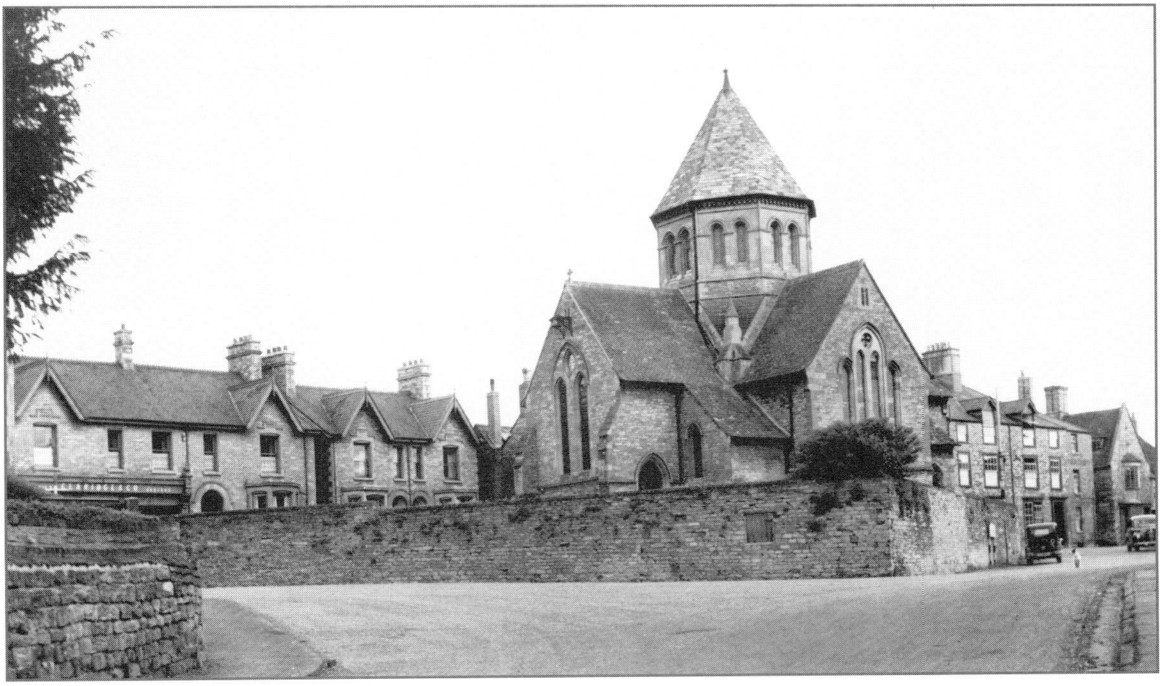

Oundle, Stoke Hill c1955 O103026
This view is little changed today, though cars now seem to lack the old scarcity value and style that we see here. Inevitably, Claridge & Co Grocers have gone, but there is still much choice of shops further into town.

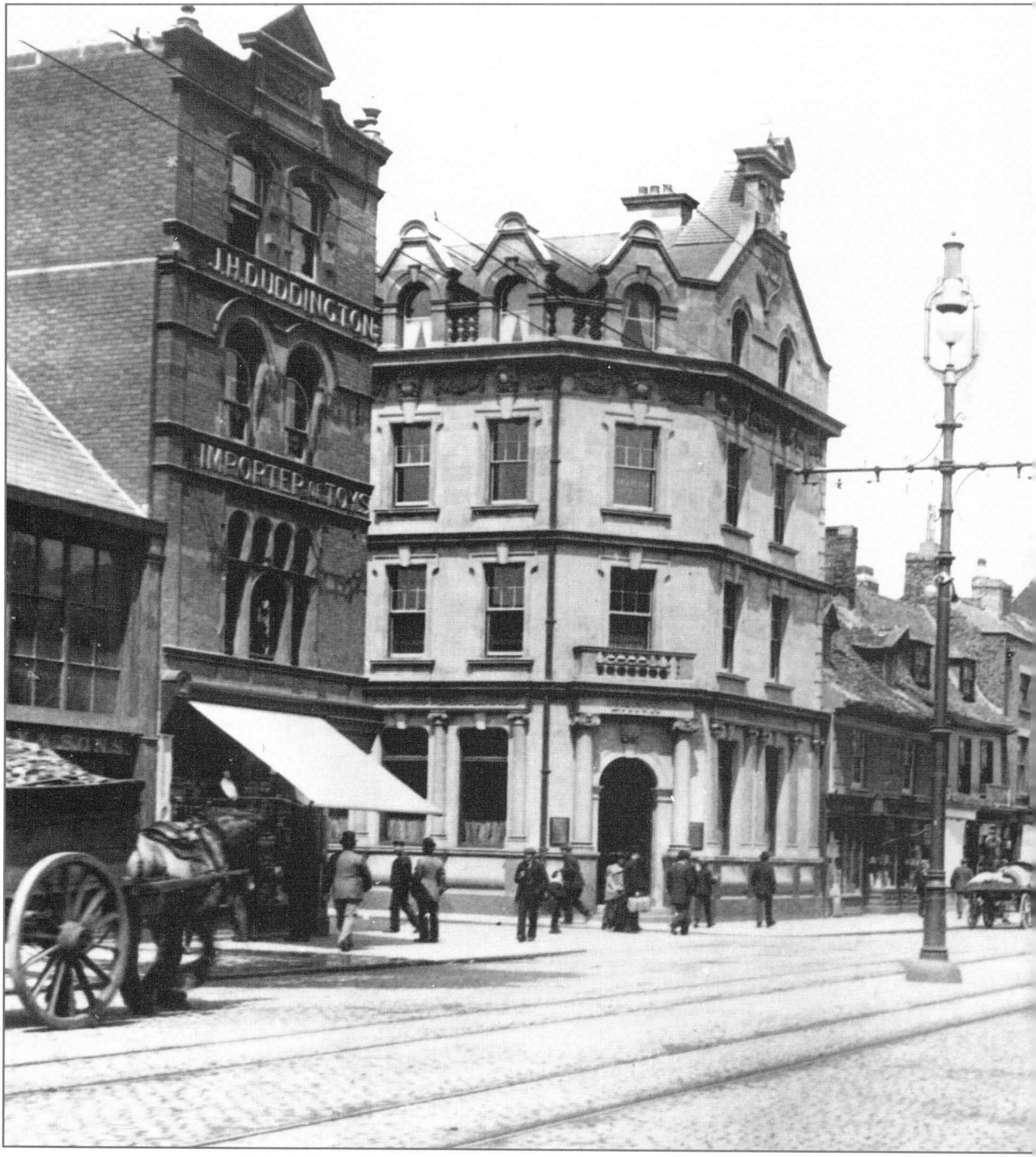

Long Causeway 1904 51547
Long Causeway is thronged with bustling lady shoppers and men at work, and trams are going to and from the terminus near the Cathedral. A well-loaded cart, probably built locally, and a straining horse heads toward Duddington's toy shop just before Cumbergate - this had been home to the woolcombers. In the distance, on the right, are the offices of Stone's mineral waters, as we can see from the large sign.

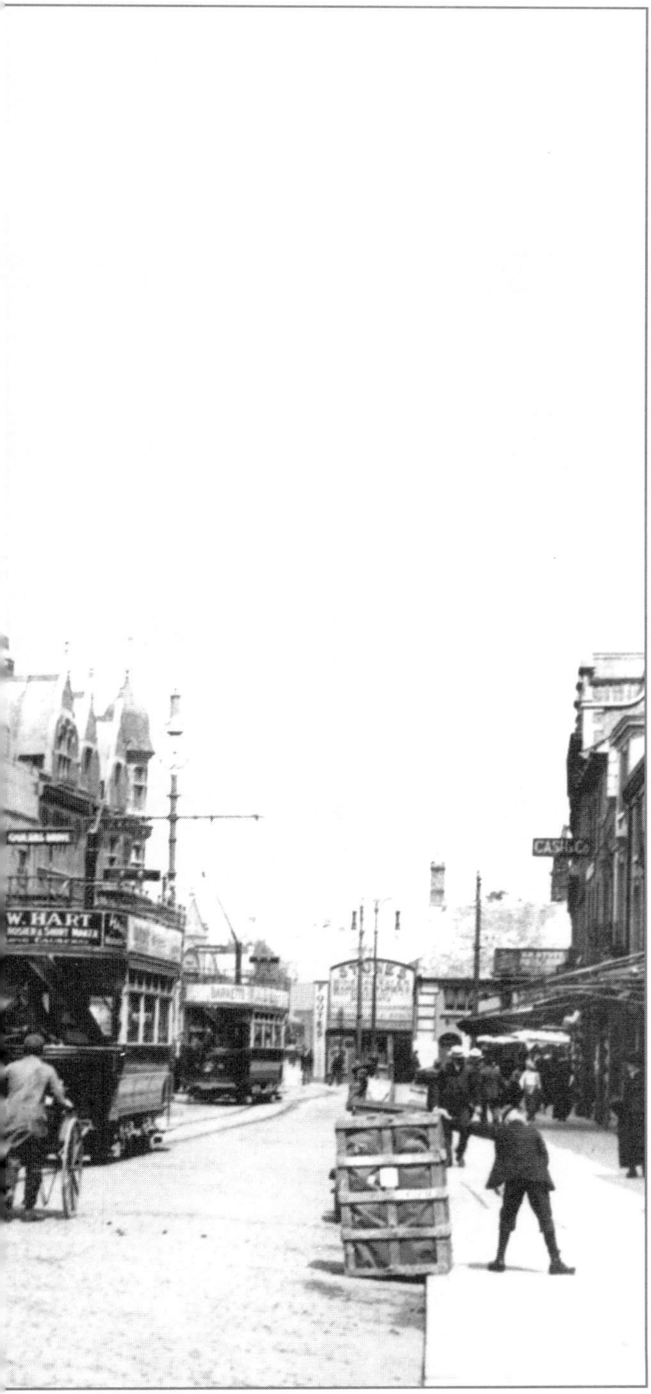

City Attractions

Peterborough, as the gateway to East Anglia, has attracted many visitors and settlers. It is a colourful and charming centre, with tall buildings old and new. They create an enclosed snug feeling around the square. Local engineers like Perkins and Royce will never be forgotten. With so many theatres in the city, there were many famous people who cast a temporary light. Fred Karno owned a theatre, the Hippodrome (now Tesco's), which drew great names to entertain the locals. Local politics has also seen much flair and dash. Charles Dickens did not like the place, and some have speculated that he used Peterborough as a model for his Eatanswill elections of 'Pickwick Papers' fame. Here he depicted a most undemocratic process in an ancient and patriotic borough, which Mr Pickwick is said to have approached via the Norwich coach. Dickens's sarcasm suggested that the people of this mighty place considered themselves of the utmost importance. Maybe they did feel high and mighty - but without such an attitude, little can be achieved. Lord Burghley served 12 years as an MP whilst devoting much time to sport; he won an Olympic Gold Medal in the 400 metre hurdles in 1928. His exploits featured in the film 'Chariots of Fire'. There ►

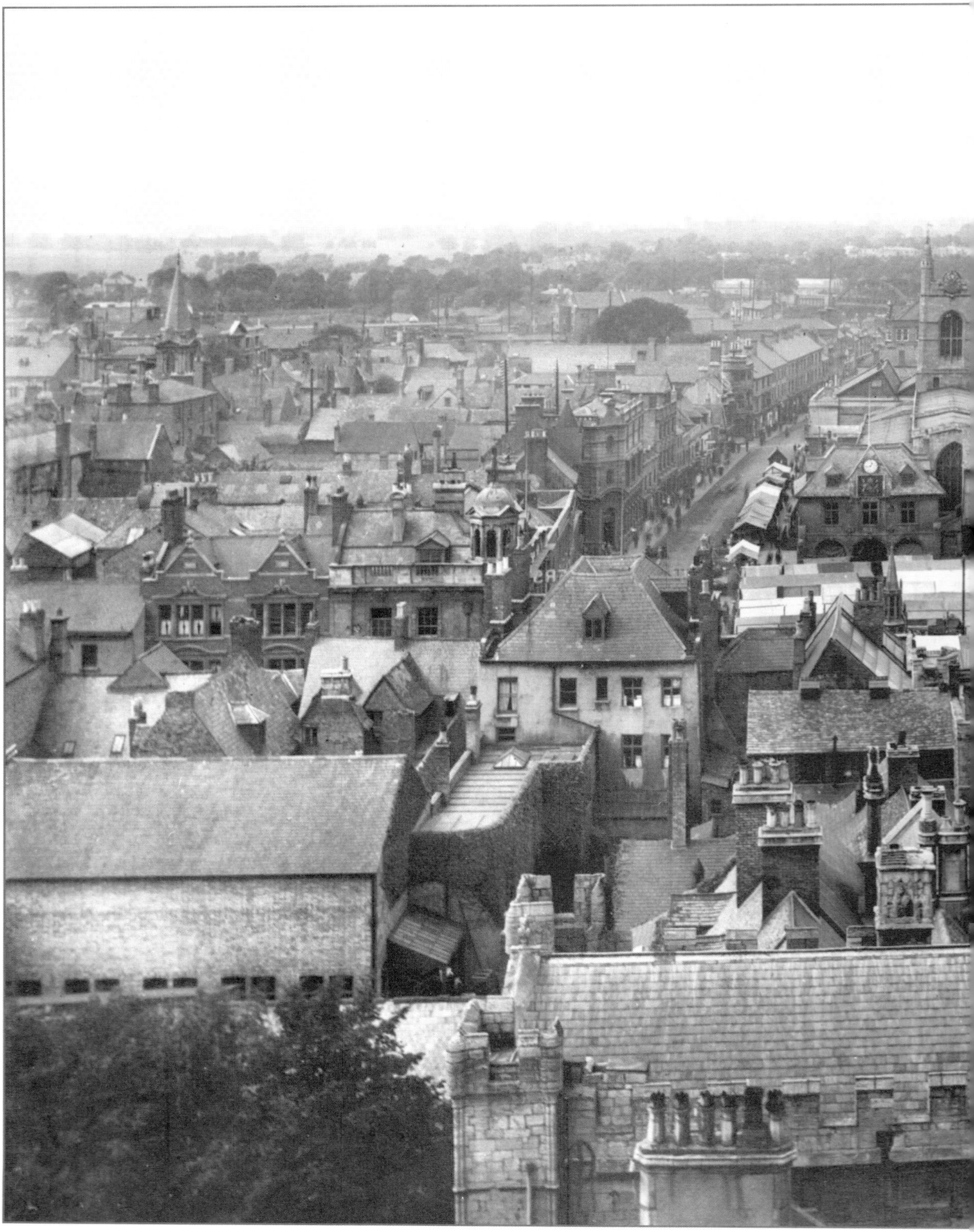

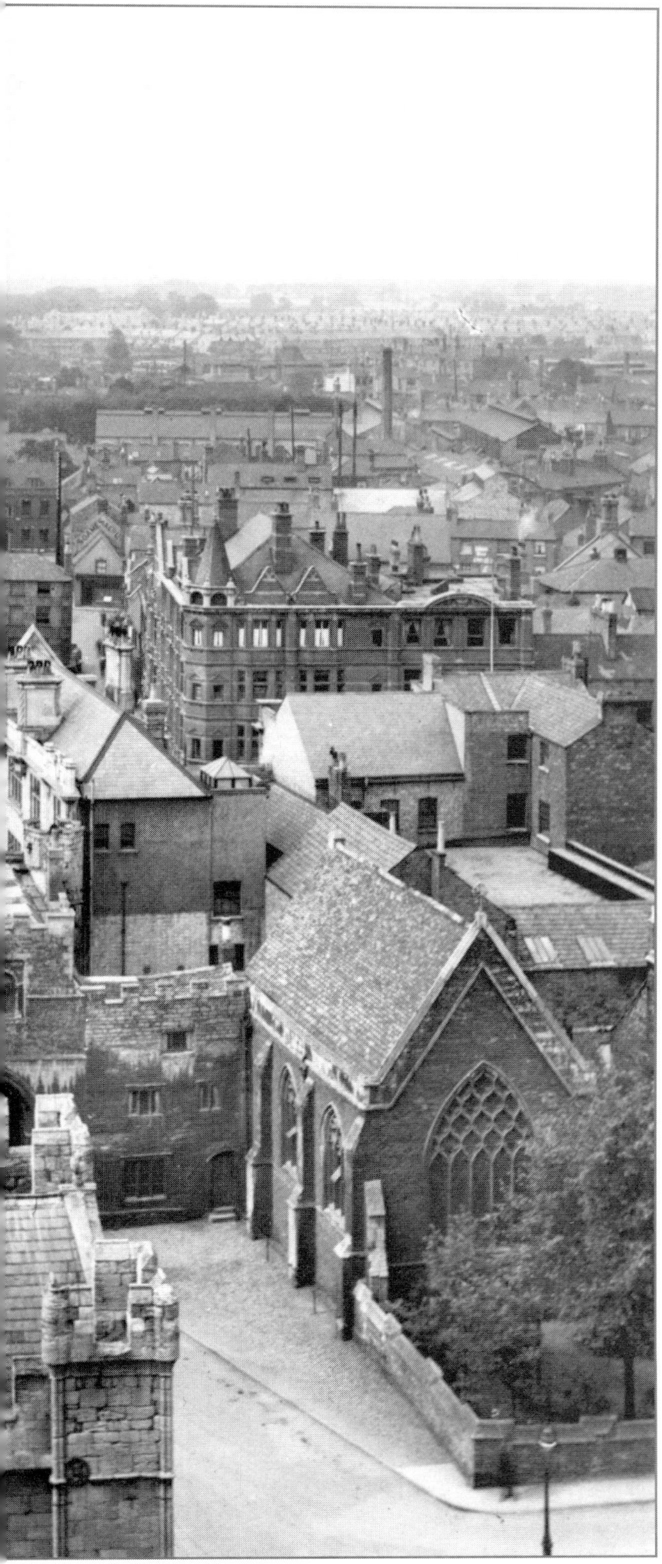

was a real chariot of fire on election night 1906. It was a Liberal landslide; the result was declared from the Guildhall, and the new member was whisked off to the Liberal club in Boroughbury. His cab was hijacked upon its return and set alight; efforts were made to push it up the Angel steps - this inn was informally the Tory HQ.

So much for the good old days. Now the main attractions are the modern shopping centres, the theatre, the river, the parks and the business parks. The old centre struggles a bit to contain the traffic, but outer development makes good use of space, and is most attractive. Everything is much bigger, faster and more convenient now.

One can imagine how impressed a young village girl, Hermione Longton, felt coming here on holidays with her grandparents during the 1950s: 'We stayed in New England, near Brotherhood's works. Grandfather belonged to their social club. They took us by coach to the pantomime every year and gave us an apple and orange when we got back. We'd lay in bed in one of those little back to backs near the railway, listening to the shunting, clanking and dropping of chains. There was so much noise with Lincoln Road on one side and the railway on the other, ▶

General View 1919 69080
This roof top scene looks west from the Cathedral. Densely-packed buildings look a little grim in monochrome, perhaps. One needs imagination to recapture the colours and sounds of that old market in progress down there in front of the Guildhall.

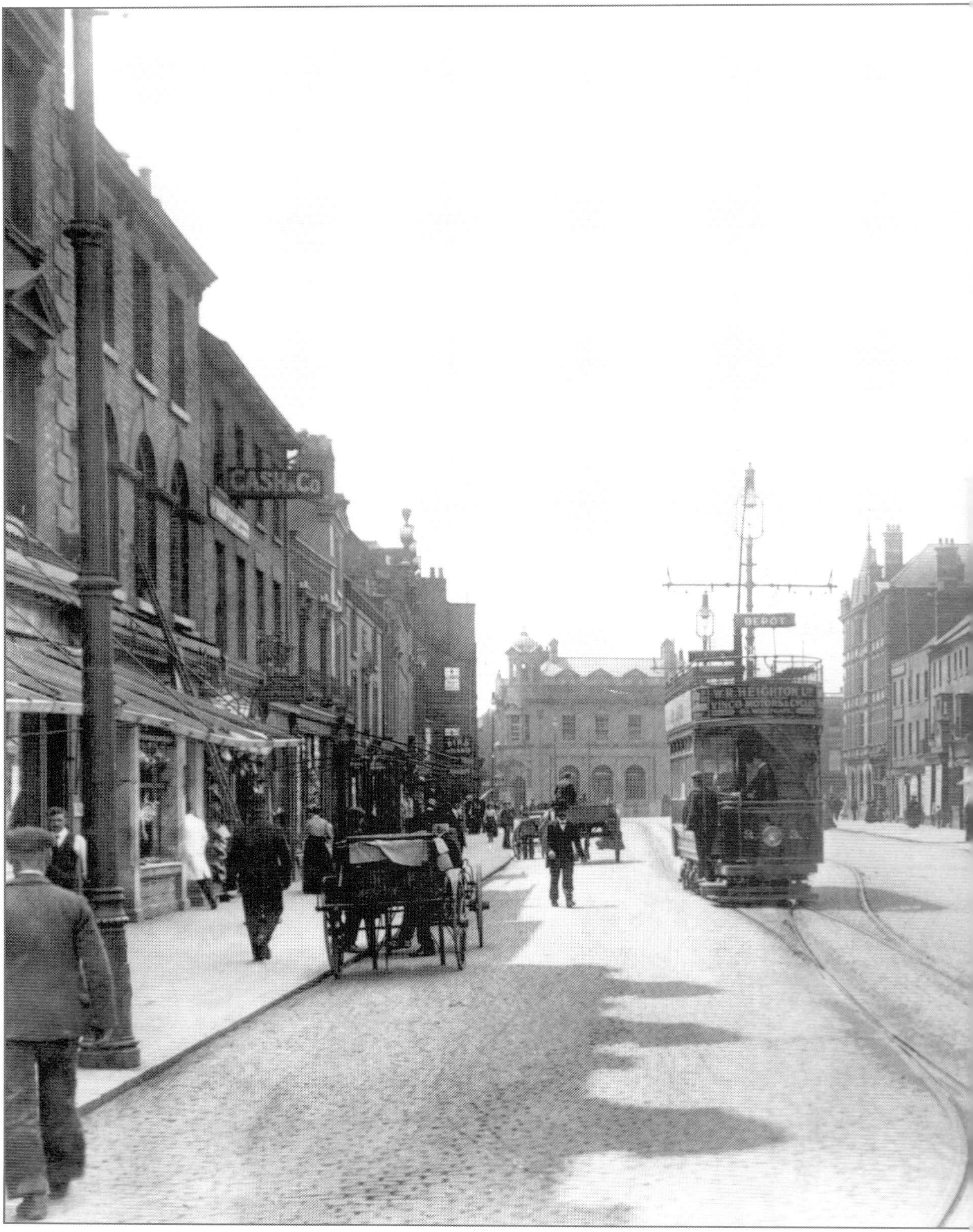
CASH&Co
DEPOT

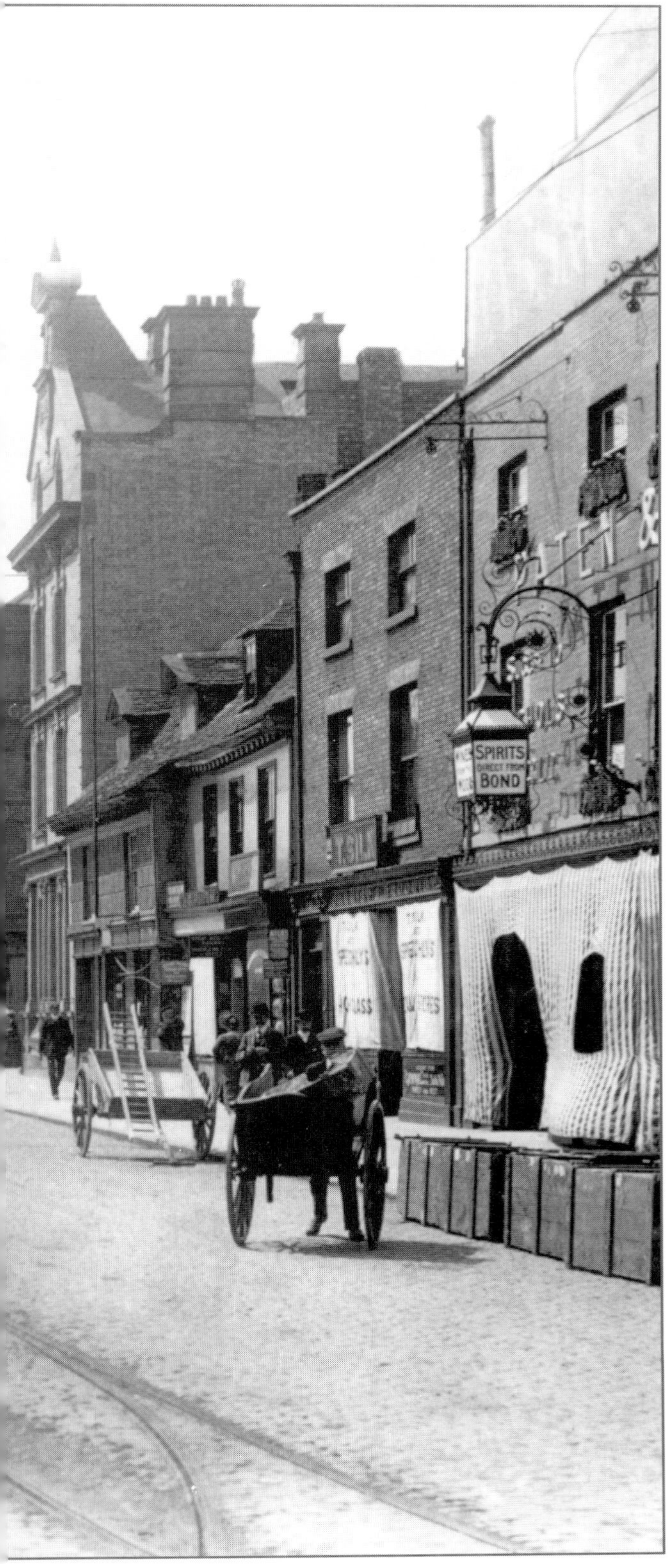

and the smell of gas mantles being lit'.

So much of the old has gone; it could never have coped with modern demands and numbers. The municipality has grown rapidly since 1921. The Local Government Act of 1972 ended the old borough, and created a large district in its place, incorporating the old Soke and extending into Cambridgeshire and Huntingdonshire. Borough status was granted in 1974, and a charter was granted to increase city responsibilities. A bright future was assured.

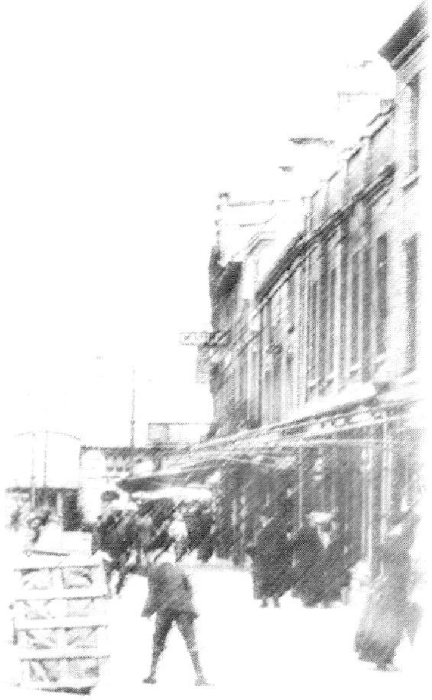

Long Causeway 1904 51547

Long Causeway 1904 51549

Trams are no longer an attraction in Peterborough, although world-wide there has been a revival, so who knows? But we will certainly never see street life like this again. Looking at Car No 3 arriving at the Long Causeway Terminus, we can see the entrance to Narrow Street directly ahead. Among the shops are Paten & Co, offering 'Spirits direct from Bond', and Cash & Co are on hand to sell the footwear. There is a lot more tiny detail here, depicting an age of much more manual effort.

The River and the Embankment c1955 P47028
The River Nene is wide and calm here; at this time, England was busy rebuilding and looking to a brighter future.

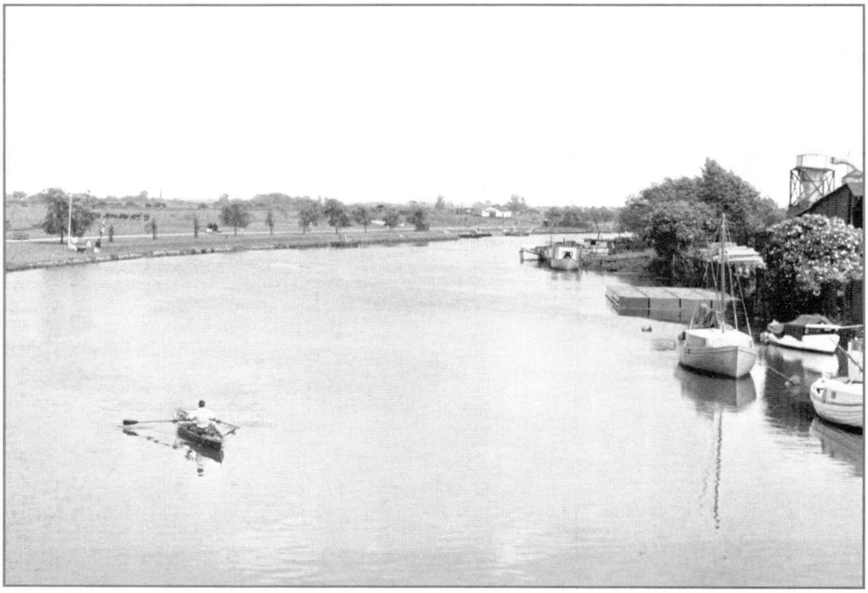

Bishop's Road Gardens 1904 51557
This picture shows a world of long ago, when feudal order had yet to fall, and higher powers decided what was and was not allowed - as the simple sign about dogs informs us. We are looking north toward the Cathedral.

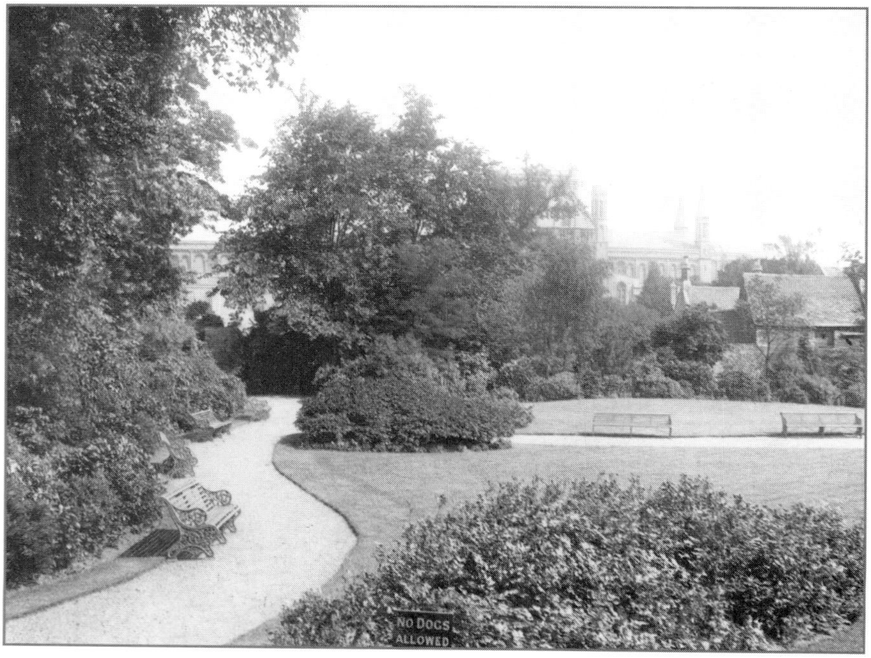

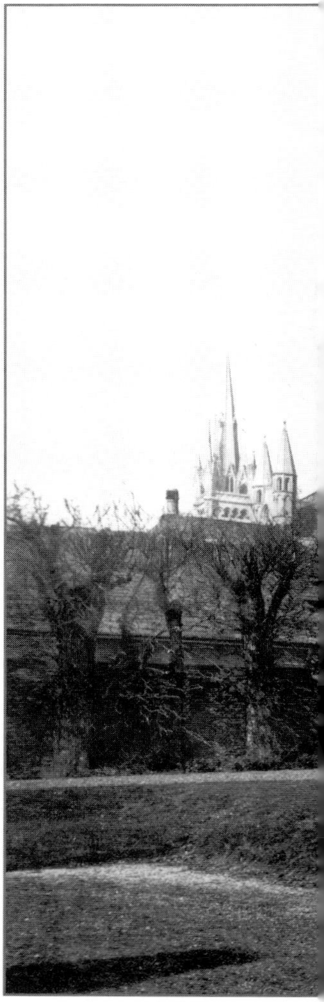

The Cathedral from the South-East 1890
24436
A final view of the Cathedral in all its glory. So much has changed around the world, but St Peter's lives on, looking solid as a rock.

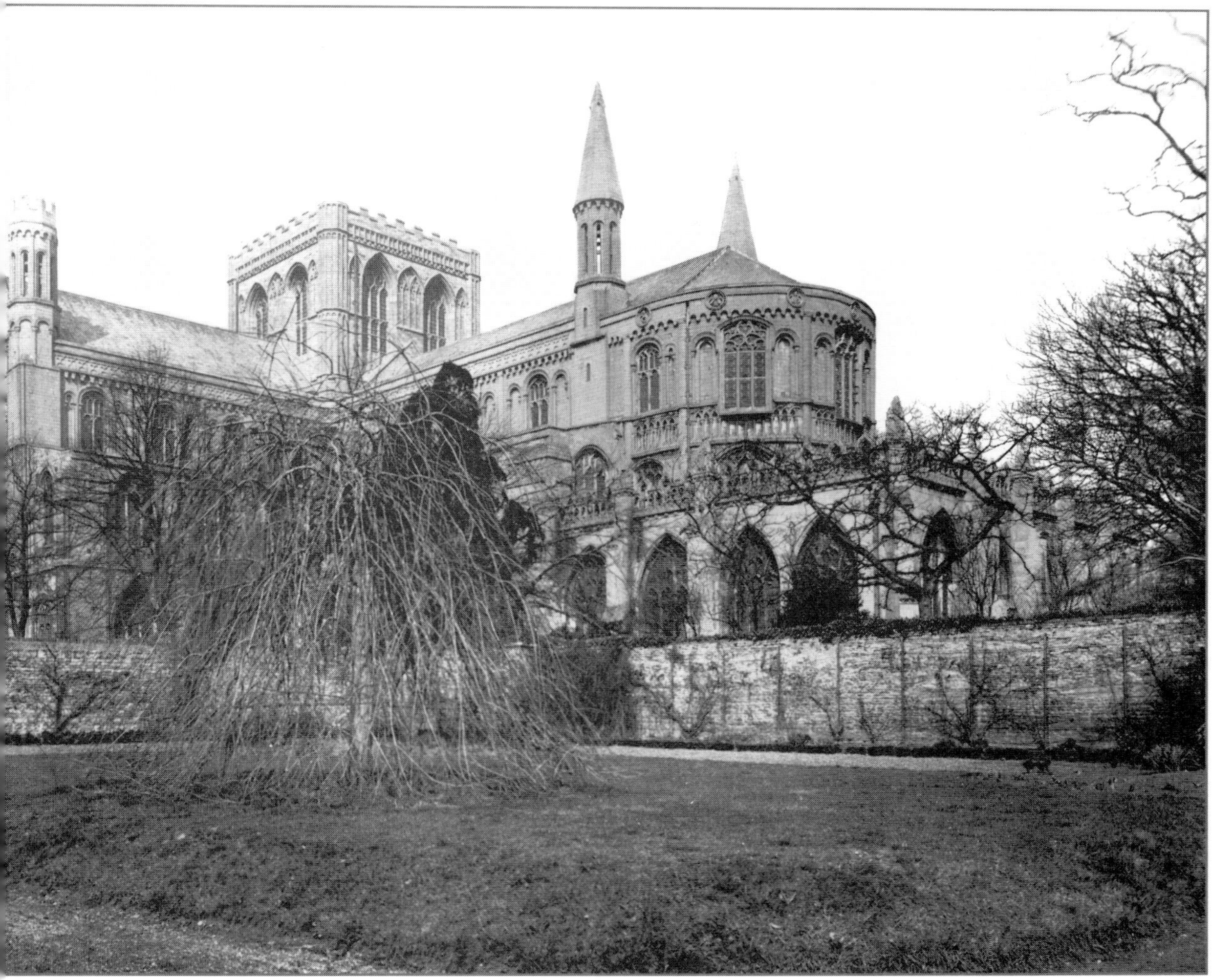

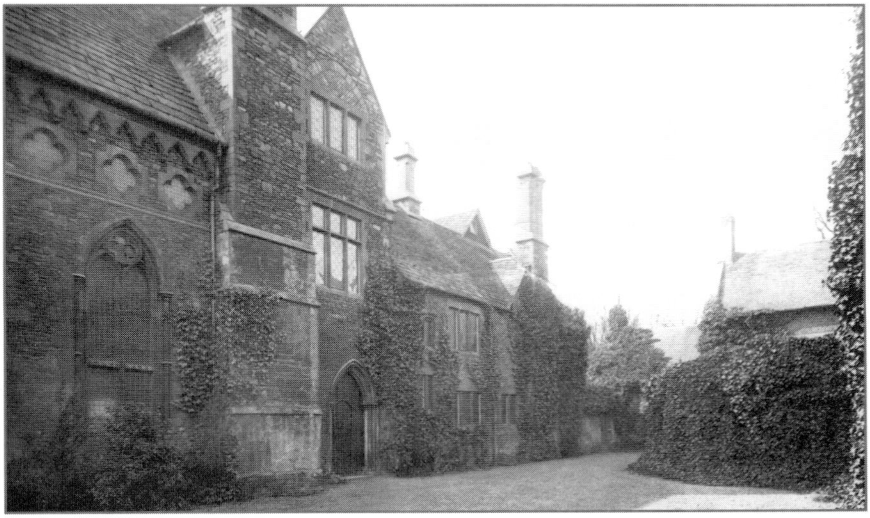

The Old Infirmary 1890
24450
This building exemplifies the fine craftsmanship that in those days earned little pecuniary reward, but gave dignity to the craftsmen and pleasure to those with time to dwell upon it - an attraction of the highest order.

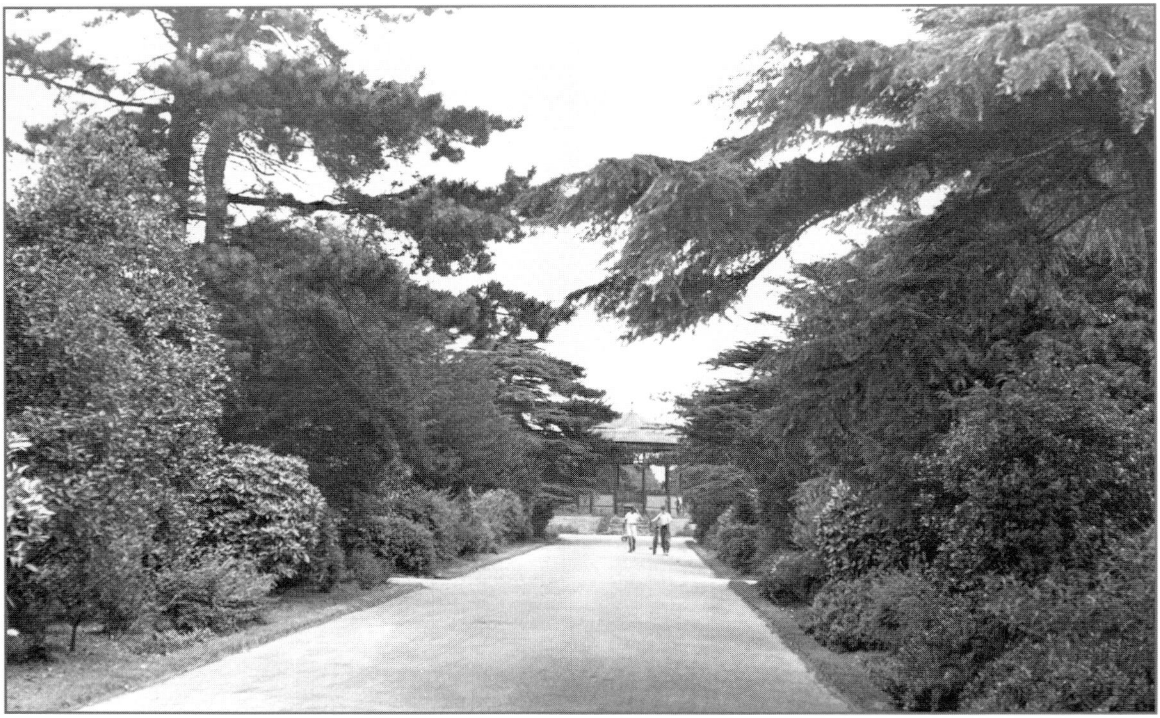

City Park c1960 P47050

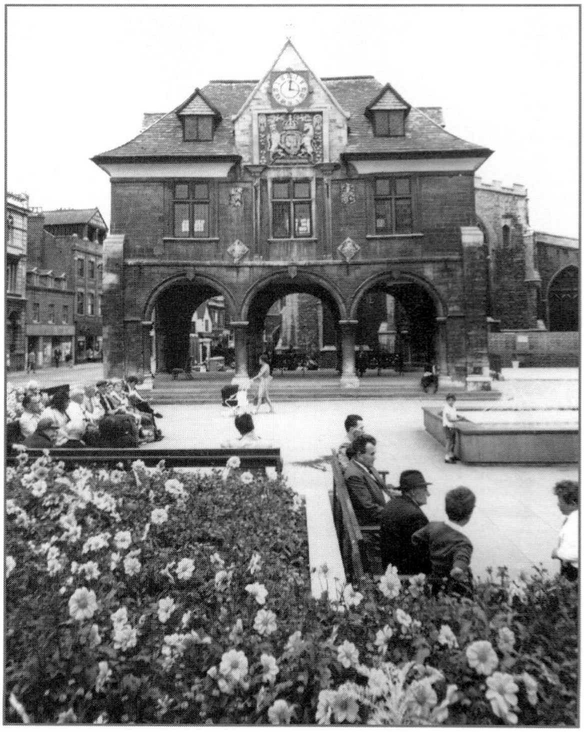

The Guildhall c1965 P47078

City Park c1960
The nation will soon be swinging, but just now it's time for simple things like strolling among the foliage.

The Guildhall c1965
This fitting final image shows folk reposing outside the Guildhall, beside the flower beds; nature and mankind are at peace in each other's company.

Index

Frith Book Co Titles

www.frithbook.co.uk

The Frith Book Company publishes over 100 new titles each year. A selection of those currently available are listed below. For latest catalogue please contact Frith Book Co.

Town Books 96pp, 100 photos. County and Themed Books 128pp, 150 photos (unless specified). All titles hardback laminated case and jacket except those indicated pb (paperback)

Around Bakewell	1-85937-113-2	£12.99
Around Barnstaple	1-85937-084-5	£12.99
Around Bath	1-85937-097-7	£12.99
Berkshire (pb)	1-85937-191-4	£9.99
Around Blackpool	1-85937-049-7	£12.99
Around Bognor Regis	1-85937-055-1	£12.99
Around Bournemouth	1-85937-067-5	£12.99
Brighton (pb)	1-85937-192-2	£8.99
British Life A Century Ago	1-85937-103-5	£17.99
Buckinghamshire (pb)	1-85937-200-7	£9.99
Around Cambridge	1-85937-092-6	£12.99
Cambridgeshire	1-85937-086-1	£14.99
Canals and Waterways	1-85937-129-9	£17.99
Cheshire	1-85937-045-4	£14.99
Around Chester	1-85937-090-x	£12.99
Around Chichester	1-85937-089-6	£12.99
Churches of Berkshire	1-85937-170-1	£17.99
Churches of Dorset	1-85937-172-8	£17.99
Colchester (pb)	1-85937-188-4	£8.99
Cornwall	1-85937-054-3	£14.99
Cumbria	1-85937-101-9	£14.99
Dartmoor	1-85937-145-0	£14.99
Around Derby	1-85937-046-2	£12.99
Derbyshire (pb)	1-85937-196-5	£9.99
Devon	1-85937-052-7	£14.99
Dorset	1-85937-075-6	£14.99
Dorset Coast	1-85937-062-4	£14.99
Down the Severn	1-85937-118-3	£14.99
Down the Thames	1-85937-121-3	£14.99
Around Dublin	1-85937-058-6	£12.99
East Sussex	1-85937-130-2	£14.99
Around Eastbourne	1-85937-061-6	£12.99
Edinburgh (pb)	1-85937-193-0	£8.99
English Castles	1-85937-078-0	£14.99
Essex	1-85937-082-9	£14.99
Around Exeter	1-85937-126-4	£12.99
Exmoor	1-85937-132-9	£14.99
Around Falmouth	1-85937-066-7	£12.99
Around Great Yarmouth	1-85937-085-3	£12.99
Around Guildford	1-85937-117-5	£12.99
Hampshire	1-85937-064-0	£14.99
Around Harrogate	1-85937-112-4	£12.99
Around Horsham	1-85937-127-2	£12.99
Around Ipswich	1-85937-133-7	£12.99
Ireland (pb)	1-85937-181-7	£9.99
Isle of Man	1-85937-065-9	£14.99
Isle of Wight	1-85937-114-0	£14.99
Kent (pb)	1-85937-189-2	£9.99
Around Leicester	1-85937-073-x	£12.99
Leicestershire (pb)	1-85937-185-x	£9.99
Around Lincoln	1-85937-111-6	£12.99
Lincolnshire	1-85937-135-3	£14.99
London (pb)	1-85937-183-3	£9.99
Around Maidstone	1-85937-056-x	£12.99
New Forest	1-85937-128-0	£14.99
Around Newark	1-85937-105-1	£12.99
Around Newquay	1-85937-140-x	£12.99
North Devon Coast	1-85937-146-9	£14.99
Northumberland and Tyne & Wear	1-85937-072-1	£14.99
Norwich (pb)	1-85937-194-9	£8.99
Around Nottingham	1-85937-060-8	£12.99
Nottinghamshire (pb)	1-85937-187-6	£9.99
Around Oxford	1-85937-096-9	£12.99
Oxfordshire	1-85937-076-4	£14.99
Peak District	1-85937-100-0	£14.99
Around Penzance	1-85937-069-1	£12.99
Around Plymouth	1-85937-119-1	£12.99
Around St Ives	1-85937-068-3	£12.99
Around Scarborough	1-85937-104-3	£12.99
Scotland (pb)	1-85937-182-5	£9.99
Scottish Castles	1-85937-077-2	£14.99
Around Sevenoaks and Tonbridge	1-85937-057-8	£12.99
Around Southampton	1-85937-088-8	£12.99
Around Southport	1-85937-106-x	£12.99

Available from your local bookshop or from the publisher

Frith Book Co Titles (continued)

Scottish Castles	1-85937-077-2	£14.99
Around Sevenoaks and Tonbridge	1-85937-057-8	£12.99
Around Southampton	1-85937-088-8	£12.99
Around Southport	1-85937-106-x	£12.99
Around Shrewsbury	1-85937-110-8	£12.99
Shropshire	1-85937-083-7	£14.99
South Devon Coast	1-85937-107-8	£14.99
South Devon Living Memories	1-85937-168-x	£14.99
Staffordshire (96pp)	1-85937-047-0	£12.99
Stone Circles & Ancient Monuments	1-85937-143-4	£17.99
Around Stratford upon Avon	1-85937-098-5	£12.99
Sussex (pb)	1-85937-184-1	£9.99
Around Torbay	1-85937-063-2	£12.99
Around Truro	1-85937-147-7	£12.99
Victorian & Edwardian Kent	1-85937-149-3	£14.99
Victorian & Edwardian Maritime Album	1-85937-144-2	£17.99
Victorian & Edwardian Yorkshire	1-85937-154-x	£14.99
Victorian Seaside	1-85937-159-0	£17.99
Warwickshire (pb)	1-85937-203-1	£9.99
Welsh Castles	1-85937-120-5	£14.99
West Midlands	1-85937-109-4	£14.99
West Sussex	1-85937-148-5	£14.99
Wiltshire	1-85937-053-5	£14.99
Around Winchester	1-85937-139-6	£12.99

Frith Book Co titles available Autumn 2000

Cotswolds (pb)	1-85937-230-9	£9.99	Sep
Cornish Coast	1-85937-163-9	£14.99	Sep
County Durham	1-85937-123-x	£14.99	Sep
Dorset Living Memories	1-85937-210-4	£14.99	Sep
Dublin (pb)	1-85937-231-7	£9.99	Sep
Herefordshire	1-85937-174-4	£14.99	Sep
Kent Living Memories	1-85937-125-6	£14.99	Sep
Leeds (pb)	1-85937-202-3	£9.99	Sep
Ludlow (pb)	1-85937-176-0	£9.99	Sep
Norfolk (pb)	1-85937-195-7	£9.99	Sep
North Yorks (pb)	1-85937-236-8	£9.99	Sep
Somerset	1-85937-153-1	£14.99	Sep
Surrey (pb)	1-85937-240-6	£9.99	Sep
Tees Valley & Cleveland	1-85937-211-2	£14.99	Sep
Thanet (pb)	1-85937-116-7	£9.99	Sep
Tiverton (pb)	1-85937-178-7	£9.99	Sep
Victorian and Edwardian Sussex	1-85937-157-4	£14.99	Sep
Weymouth (pb)	1-85937-209-0	£9.99	Sep
Worcestershire	1-85937-152-3	£14.99	Sep
Yorkshire Living Memories	1-85937-166-3	£14.99	Sep
British Life A Century Ago (pb)	1-85937-213-9	£9.99	Oct
Camberley (pb)	1-85937-222-8	£9.99	Oct
Cardiff (pb)	1-85937-093-4	£9.99	Oct
Carmarthenshire	1-85937-216-3	£14.99	Oct
Cheltenham (pb)	1-85937-095-0	£9.99	Oct
Cornwall (pb)	1-85937-229-5	£9.99	Oct
English Country Houses	1-85937-161-2	£17.99	Oct
Folkestone (pb)	1-85937-124-8	£9.99	Oct
Humberside	1-85937-215-5	£14.99	Oct
Manchester (pb)	1-85937-198-1	£9.99	Oct
Norfolk Living Memories	1-85937-217-1	£14.99	Oct
Preston (pb)	1-85937-212-0	£9.99	Oct
Reading (pb)	1-85937-238-4	£9.99	Oct
Salisbury (pb)	1-85937-239-2	£9.99	Oct
South Hams	1-85937-220-1	£14.99	Oct
Suffolk (pb)	1-85937-221-x	£9.99	Oct
Swansea (pb)	1-85937-167-1	£9.99	Oct
West Yorkshire (pb)	1-85937-201-5	£9.99	Oct
Around Aylesbury (pb)	1-85937-227-9	£9.99	Nov
Around Bradford (pb)	1-85937-204-x	£9.99	Nov
Around Chichester (pb)	1-85937-228-7	£9.99	Nov
East Anglia (pb)	1-85937-265-1	£9.99	Nov
East London	1-85937-080-2	£14.99	Nov
Gloucestershire	1-85937-102-7	£14.99	Nov
Greater Manchester (pb)	1-85937-266-x	£9.99	Nov
Hastings & Bexhill (pb)	1-85937-131-0	£9.99	Nov
Helston (pb)	1-85937-214-7	£9.99	Nov
Lancaster, Morecombe & Heysham (pb)	1-85937-233-3	£9.99	Nov
Peterborough (pb)	1-85937-219-8	£9.99	Nov
Piers	1-85937-237-6	£17.99	Nov
Wiltshire Living Memories	1-85937-245-7	£14.99	Nov
Windmills & Watermills	1-85937-242-2	£17.99	Nov
York (pb)	1-85937-199-x	£9.99	Nov

See Frith books on the internet www.frithbook.co.uk

FRITH PRODUCTS & SERVICES

Francis Frith would doubtless be pleased to know that the pioneering publishing venture he started in 1860 still continues today. A hundred and forty years later, The Francis Frith Collection continues in the same innovative tradition and is now one of the foremost publishers of vintage photographs in the world. Some of the current activities include:

Interior Decoration

Today Frith's photographs can be seen framed and as giant wall murals in thousands of pubs, restaurants, hotels, banks, retail stores and other public buildings throughout the country. In every case they enhance the unique local atmosphere of the places they depict and provide reminders of gentler days in an increasingly busy and frenetic world.

Product Promotions

Frith products are used by many major companies to promote the sales of their own products or to reinforce their own history and heritage. Frith promotions have been used by Hovis bread, Courage beers, Scots Porage Oats, Colman's mustard, Cadbury's foods, Mellow Birds coffee, Dunhill pipe tobacco, Guinness, and Bulmer's Cider.

Genealogy and Family History

As the interest in family history and roots grows world-wide, more and more people are turning to Frith's photographs of Great Britain for images of the towns, villages and streets where their ancestors lived; and, of course, photographs of the churches and chapels where their ancestors were christened, married and buried are an essential part of every genealogy tree and family album.

Frith Products

All Frith photographs are available Framed or just as Mounted Prints and Posters (size 23 x 16 inches). These may be ordered from the address below. From time to time other products - Address Books, Calendars, Table Mats, etc - are available.

The Internet

Already twenty thousand Frith photographs can be viewed and purchased on the internet. By the end of the year 2000 some 60,000 Frith photographs will be available on the internet. The number of sites is constantly expanding, each focussing on different products and services from the Collection.
The main Frith sites are listed below.

www.francisfrith.co.uk
www.frithbook.co.uk

See the complete list of Frith Books at:

www.frithbook.co.uk

This web site is regularly updated with the latest list of publications from the Frith Book Company. If you wish to buy books relating to another part of the country that your local bookshop does not stock, you may purchase on-line.

For further information, trade, or author enquiries please contact us at the address below:

The Francis Frith Collection, Frith's Barn, Teffont, Salisbury, Wiltshire, England SP3 5QP.
Tel: +44 (0)1722 716 376 Fax: +44 (0)1722 716 881 Email: uksales@francisfrith.com

See Frith books on the internet www.frithbook.co.uk

TO RECEIVE YOUR FREE MOUNTED PRINT

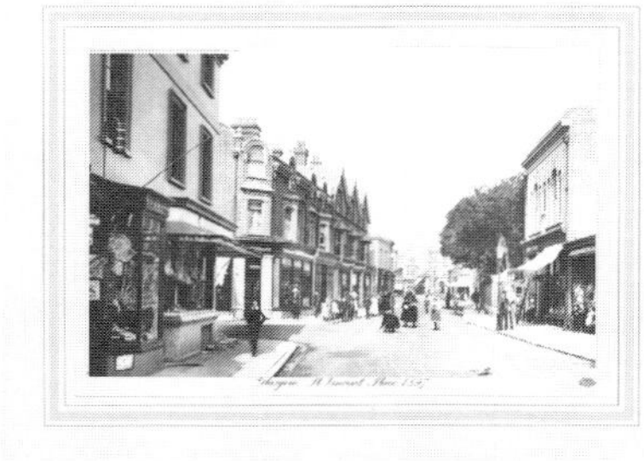

Mounted Print
Overall size 14 x 11 inches

Cut out this Voucher and return it with your remittance for £1.50 to cover postage and handling, to UK addresses. For overseas addresses please include £4.00 post and handling.
Choose any photograph included in this book. Your SEPIA print will be A4 in size, and mounted in a cream mount with burgundy rule lines, overall size 14 x 11 inches.

Order additional Mounted Prints at HALF PRICE (only £7.49 each*)
If there are further pictures you would like to order, possibly as gifts for friends and family, purchase them at half price (no additional postage and handling required).

Have your Mounted Prints framed*
For an additional £14.95 per print you can have your chosen Mounted Print framed in an elegant polished wood and gilt moulding, overall size 16 x 13 inches (no additional postage and handling required).

*** IMPORTANT!**
These special prices are only available if ordered using the original voucher on this page (no copies permitted) and at the same time as your free Mounted Print, for delivery to the same address

Frith Collectors' Guild

From time to time we publish a magazine of news and stories about Frith photographs and further special offers of Frith products. If you would like 12 months FREE membership, please return this form.

Send completed forms to:
The Francis Frith Collection, Frith's Barn, Teffont, Salisbury, Wiltshire SP3 5QP

Voucher for FREE and Reduced Price Frith Prints

Picture no.	Page number	Qty	Mounted @ £7.49	Framed + £14.95	Total Cost
		1	**Free of charge***	£	£
			£7.49	£	£
			£7.49	£	£
			£7.49	£	£
			£7.49	£	£
			£7.49	£	£
Please allow 28 days for delivery			*** Post & handling**		**£1.50**
Book Title			**Total Order Cost**		**£**

Please do not photocopy this voucher. Only the original is valid, so please cut it out and return it to us.

I enclose a cheque / postal order for £ ....
made payable to 'The Francis Frith Collection'
OR please debit my Mastercard / Visa / Switch / Amex card
(credit cards please on all overseas orders)

Number ....
Issue No (Switch only) .... Valid from (Amex/Switch) ....
Expires .... Signature ....

Name Mr/Mrs/Ms ....
Address ....
....
....
.... Postcode ....
Daytime Tel No .... Valid to 31/12/02

The Francis Frith Collectors' Guild

Please enrol me as a member for 12 months free of charge.

Name Mr/Mrs/Ms ....
Address ....
....
....
.... Postcode ....